UNASHAMED

UNASHAMED

Musings of a Fat, Black Muslim

LEAH VERNON

BEACON PRESS ■ BOSTON

Beacon Press
Boston, Massachusetts
www.beacon.org

Beacon Press books
are published under the auspices of
the Unitarian Universalist Association of Congregations.

23 22 21 20   8 7 6 5 4 3 2 1

This book is printed on acid-free paper that meets the uncoated paper
ANSI/NISO specifications for permanence as revised in 1992.

Text design and composition by Kim Arney

Library of Congress Cataloging-in-Publication Data

Names: Vernon, Leah, author.
Title: Unashamed : musings of a fat, black Muslim / Leah Vernon.
Description: Boston : Beacon Press, [2019]
Identifiers: LCCN 2019023425 (print) | LCCN 2019023426 (ebook) | ISBN
9780807002681 (paperback) | ISBN 9780807012635 (ebook)
Subjects: LCSH: Vernon, Leah. | Muslim women—United States—Biography. |
African American Muslims—Biography. | Body image in women. | Feminism.
Classification: LCC E184.M88 V47 2019 (print) | LCC E184.M88 (ebook) |
DDC 305.48/6970092 [B]—dc23
LC record available at https://lccn.loc.gov/2019023425
LC ebook record available at https://lccn.loc.gov/2019023426

To all those who are struggling
to find the uniqueness in their beauty

CONTENTS

PART 5: UNAPOLOGETICALLY ME

PREFACE

I'm a fat, Black, Muslim woman from Detroit.

And where I come from, women hide things. My family, my people, have been hiding all their lives. My great-grandmother took my great-grandfather's identity to the grave. A piece of the past, our past, gone in the wind.

We hide molestation, child abuse, spousal abuse. We conceal mental illness and eating disorders. We hide illegitimate children, abortion, and drug abuse. Most of us sit on information and hide behind computer screens and pretend to be people that we aren't. When our husbands cheat with strippers, we smile and give greetings. When we are attacked by Islamophobes, we hug and pray. When we hurt, we conceal. *Hide the trauma. Hide the pain. Don't say a word. Don't be ungrateful. There are bigger problems in this world. You are one of the lucky ones.*

When I first started writing, I planned to write under a pen name. I didn't want anyone to know me—a Muslim woman, writing about things I shouldn't. I was going to embarrass myself, my husband, my friends, and my religion. In my mind, I'd be a complete disgrace.

I allowed white sensitivity to dictate what I said and how I said it. When there was a social justice issue, I zipped my lips, not allowing myself to participate in the hush-hush conversation going on among my people of color.

Feminism? What was that? I couldn't be a feminist because I was married. I was Muslim. Certain kinds of women empowerment made certain men uncomfortable.

Seems like when you're born with a vagina, stereotypes and ceilings and walls and fortresses are instantaneously built around you. Society says that my body is too fat, too curvy, too lumpy. Why do I have to be constantly policed? *Your teeth are fucked. Go buy a new grill. No lashes? Buy some. Pile your face with makeup and you're fake. If you don't, then you're not a lady. You're not feminine enough.*

As soon as they stamp your birth certificate with a minority race, it's only downhill from there. You will always, always, be judged. If it's natural or on a Black face, then it's deemed unworthy. *Your lips are too big, but big is okay for a white girl whose lips are poked and injected. Your hair is too nappy; just perm it or put on a blonde wig so that you resemble a white girl.*

Same thing with religion: *Take off the scarf. It means you're oppressed by a man. It makes Americans feel more comfortable with you if you don't wear it, no longer rep for Islam. You want to get on birth control? Can't do that. That's not what God intended.*

When I walk into a room, it seems all people see is my hijab. Then my Black face. Then my obese body. Through all of my trials and tribulations, my existence has been reduced to two choices: be myself or allow the world to dictate who I am.

For too long, I've allowed the world to dictate. And now, we are here. Right at this very moment. I'm sharing some things that I've never, ever shared with my close friends. I'm exposing myself. What I was and who I am now. Although, *exposing* is such a negative word.

To me, I am freeing myself.

The day I let go of the heaviness of how the world viewed me was the day I let myself go.

I'm not a poster child for anything. Please don't deem me as this or that. I am me. Solely me. With my own opinions and skewed outlooks and quirks. I'm not seeking validation nor am I seeking a pat on the back.

With these stories, I want you to learn. Heal. Think outside the box. Disengage from groupthink. Detach from the ideology that people, humans, can be stuffed into a nice little circle with a polka-dot bow on top. I don't care what people post, how amazing their photos look, or how their husbands have that perfect jawline. We are all humans with complexities. We are equal. We are fucked up. But we are beautiful and interesting and knowledgeable.

And we all have a story to tell.

PART 1
GOOD MUSLIM GIRL

■ ■ ■ ■ ■ ■ ■ ■ ■

1. THE SHIRT THAT SWALLOWED ME WHOLE

When Mom noticed that I was "filling in," she no longer allowed me to pick out my own clothes. She'd take us to one of her favorite spots, Mammoth, a department store that sold irregular-sized socks and undershirts.

We lived in an era of baby-tees that hung just above the belly button, neck chokers, embellished jeans, and slip dresses. I wanted in. But I couldn't really get in-in because Muslim girls are only allowed to show their hands, feet, and face. The rest has to be covered to practice modesty.

Little Sister went first. Mom picked colorful shirts for her with sparkles and unicorns and other cutesy embroideries on them. Mom was in a good mood because she had a little money in her pocket since it was tax time, so I was going to try to convince her—without telling on myself because we weren't allowed to watch anything over the PG rating due to sexual conduct in many of the movies that Mom deemed inappropriate for our young Muslim minds—to let me mimic a few styles from the movie *Clueless*.

I stood in the middle of the juniors' section with all the newest styles. They even had hip-hugger bell-bottoms. There were racks upon racks of jeans in different colors. I grabbed a pair, sucked in my stomach, and put it up to my waist. They were cute but barely covered my fat legs. I peeked inside the jeans and pulled out the tag. Size eight. Wtf? Well, not wtf because that's a newer saying. It was more like, what da heck!

I needed to find my size and searched for the double-digit rack. I doubled back. Every rack ended at a size twelve. Not a real size twelve but a size twelve in juniors. Which was basically like two sizes too small.

Panicking, I searched again. Maybe I'd missed that lonely rack with slightly extended sizes. I could've squeezed into something. I could've lost weight or cut off a part of my thigh. I was going to make a pair of jeans in that department store work.

Time passed and "Operation Find Plus-Size Jeans" was a complete fail. I figured that if they didn't have jeans, then maybe they had shirts in my size. I didn't have much boob, so how hard could it be?

The shirts were also made tiny, but it was fine because I could just stuff my rolls into a size large. I was big, but I wasn't that big.

I snatched a cute stretchy, tie-dye shirt with long sleeves off the hanger and rushed to the full-body mirror by the dressing rooms. I burst into an empty room and tore off my shirt. I pulled the new shirt over my head. So far, so good. But then—see what had happened was, as I tried to put my arms into the sleeves, the fat got caught. The stretch of the shirt had reached its maximum stretch capacity. I looked in the mirror and stared at the stuffed human sausage staring back. The double chin peeking over the soft neckline and the belly roll resting over my too big distressed jeans.

Mom called my name. I carefully placed the cute little shirt that I couldn't fit back on the hanger and met up with Mom and Little Sister, who was happily hanging off the side of the shopping cart filled with clothes.

"Come on," Mom said.

I took the walk of shame to the men's department, dragging my Payless brand sneakers along the dull tile. Mom parked her cart near the T-shirt rack and dove in.

"Stand up straight and put your arms out," Mom said, as she held up a very long T-shirt.

She put it up to my chest and allowed it to fall down to my knees. I couldn't have explained how my face looked. I was pretty good at hiding my emotions, but I knew for sure that gloom was written all over it.

"Turn around," she ordered.

I twisted around with slumped shoulders. She did the same thing to the back of me and allowed the shapeless shirt to fall. "Good. Your butt is covered."

I glared at the ugly red shirt that would probably look better on a tree trunk. She laid the monstrosity on top of Little Sister's pretty clothes. Mom continued to go up and down the aisle and chose different colors of the same kind of shirt: an ugly blue one and an ugly black one were added to the pile with the ugly red one. All big. All shapeless, but modest to her Muslim mother mind. I was never going to get to be like any of the characters in *Clueless*: no cool after-school parties or '90s montages, or making out with a high school boy in the back of a really cool convertible that my white dad gave me for my sixteenth birthday.

I'm not saying that she should've allowed me to wear booty shorts and itty-bitty tees so I could fit in, but bedsheets aren't cool! I also got that we were Muslim, and Muslim women during puberty are supposed to dress modestly and cover their hair, but shouldn't it have been a choice? Wouldn't it have made more sense to explain, then give the option? Yeah, I was a dumb thirteen-year-old, but I felt as though she'd already made up her mind that I was going to dress modestly because she said so. Which was fine, but kids are oh-so-clever, and during adolescence, we figure out ways to do what the hell we want.

I was clever.

Oh, Mom didn't let me wear those tight jeans with the rips in the knee? I took my allowance, pretended to ride my bike to 7-Eleven, but really took a detour to the strip mall, and bought those jeans anyway, stuffed them in my backpack, snuck them upstairs to my room, and plotted another plan on how I could wear them to the mall with my friend.

I had one idea of who I wanted to be in this world, while she, on the other hand, had another.

■ ■ ■ ■

While Mom was trying to figure out who each of her children should be, she was also trying to figure out who she was as a young and newly Muslim mother with five children—three girls and two boys—by five different fathers. Mom married many, many times. That's putting it lightly—and no, I'm not including her "man-friends" or fiancés. Mom never married my older sister's father or mine. My dad was a man-whore who just wanted a young thang, and she probably subconsciously wanted a daddy figure. My sister's father was a criminal, always in and out of jail. No one ever knew where he was, but one could assume, in police custody. My younger brother's father was her first real husband. His family was Muslim, and from him, Mom got her first exposure to Islam. Until then, her life was surrounded by diluted Christianity. You know the kind, where you just go to church sometimes and participate on holidays. She never connected with it.

Mom converted to Islam before getting married. I was maybe six-ish when it happened, and my older sister was a preteen. I recall that Mom stopped drinking and started wearing the hijab. She was becoming a better person. Leading up to the marriage, he and Mom knew each other from the neighborhood. Her family didn't care for him, mainly because he was known as a troublemaker. He and his brothers used to run the streets and try to sic their pit bulls on white people. They grew up on the belief, like a number of Nation of Islam Muslims at the time had, that the white man was the devil.

My brother's father was tall and light-skinned, with a face covered with freckles. Mom said he was handsome. He didn't have any kids at the time, like Mom had. The sad part was that he also came from an unstable family background similar to Mom's. And two broken people can't fix each other.

I can't remember much from that time, but three memories have stuck. The first one was riding on a Jeep Power Wheels with my twin step-siblings. I sat in the back seat, and they refused to let me take the wheel. Although sad, I was excited to just be there. Power Wheels were all the rage at that time, and Mom couldn't afford fancy toys like that, so I basked in the fun while it lasted. The second was when I choked on a piece of hard candy, and my biological dad came from behind like the angel he is not and pumped my little belly until the candy flew out onto the lawn. I remembered almost dying. My little lungs struggling to catch air. The third was domestic violence.

I remember being in the den, seemingly standing there like a fixture. My little brother's father was on one side of the room and Mom was on the other. They were screaming. Mom's arms flailed in the air, and he pointed, both trying to get their arguments across. Veins protruded from his neck. She got in his face. He shoved her. Very hard. Then she went ballistic. We had an ancient computer. The black monitor with the big, beige brain. She picked it up and heaved it at him. It missed and shattered on the hardwood floor.

I don't remember running, hiding, crying. I stood there, still, as two adults expressed hurt and anger toward one another. Maybe I wasn't scared because these outbursts were already normal to my kid brain.

After that one failed, all of Mom's husbands were also Muslim, but although different in their own ways, followed the same suit of fuckery as the first. Mom had a new man every three years and, sometimes, every other year. Just as one was departing, another was in the pipeline. Although she was very independent and outspoken, she wasn't comfortable being alone. She wanted her growing child base to have the father figure that she'd never had. She was looking for the male species to save her, fill a void that could never be filled.

Before I knew all the facets that shaped Mom, I used to wonder why it just couldn't be her and us. Were we not enough? To me, we were fine without those dudes. Most of them weren't shit anyway. But I kind of get it now. Everyone needs someone. Perhaps all of our baby faces weren't enough. Because all our baby faces would turn into adult faces. Then we'd leave, just like everyone else had.

These men, they fell in love with the idea of Mom, but sadly, none of them knew the real her. And none of them had the equipment to handle her. Hell, we could barely handle her. Her mood swings, her constant need for control. Her wrath was something to be feared. We just knew when to lay low and abort missions. Those men wanted to challenge her. Change her. And she wasn't having none of that.

Mom was tall, with a tiny waist, wide hips, and a high butt. Her eyes were dark and fierce like a panther's. Her skin was smooth like peanut butter and youthful. When I grew up, people would ask if she was my sister. That made me feel old as hell, but I believe she enjoyed the compliments. Mom was a Black chameleon. She could go into any situation and adapt seamlessly. She was sneaky and confident, yet nurturing and warm.

Others didn't see her that way. Most thought Mom was eccentric, crazy, different. But according to her, she was just protecting us from the world that she grew up in. The world that hadn't given her a chance to be good, to be pure.

Her parents were working-class people from the South who migrated to Detroit to work on the lines at the car plants like most Black folks did during the '60s and '70s. Her biological father was never present, too busy being a rolling stone and pursuing a career of shiesty gambling and God knows what else. He gave up his rights as a father and allowed her stepfather to adopt her. Mom's stepfather turned out to be abusive to not only my mom but her mother too.

Both parents were gamblers, drinkers, and partiers. She and her two younger sisters had to mostly fend for themselves at home when their parents weren't present. And somewhere, mixed in the craziness of her upbringing, she was molested.

Since life hadn't dealt her a fair hand, her so-called "crazy" was justified to me, to us children.

She played Mommy and Daddy, the weight of the world of responsibility for five little ones on her shoulders, and she never let us out of her sight. We weren't allowed to go over to anyone's house alone. We weren't allowed to go to the end of the block. We could ride our bikes only two houses down. If I was feeling rebellious, I'd take it as far as four houses. We weren't allowed to cross the street or go around the corner or ride our bikes to the liquor store like all the other kids. We couldn't go into our neighbor's house to play with their kids. We weren't allowed to eat candy or drink Kool-Aid. Sleepovers were a definite no, even if it was with one of her good Muslim lady friends who had kids our age. We couldn't stay outside when the streetlights came on, even in the winter when they came on at 5:30 p.m. We weren't allowed to talk in slang. Words like *huh, yeah,* and *shut up* were off-limits. We could only watch PG-rated movies and listen to "clean" music. Phone calls past a certain time were a no-go. Immodest clothes. No. Fantasy books and teen magazines. No. Boys, we didn't even try to ask about, for obvious reasons.

We were also homeschooled from very early on, which her family thought was very odd because no families they knew were doing that. But many Muslim children that I knew were also homeschooled. I had never stepped foot in a public school, which I started to resent as I got older and started making friends who were actually in public school. I wanted the whole high school experience. But looking back on it, had I really missed anything important?

I believe we were homeschooled for several reasons, but I think religion and her want for a controlled environment were the main two. If you want to make sure your child is immersed in a certain way of living or lifestyle, schooling is a huge part of what shapes them. In public school, we wouldn't be surrounded by Muslims or Islam or modesty or any of the values that Mom wanted for us. So, she had to create that bubble, a bubble in which she controlled the outcome. Mom hadn't wanted us fraternizing with the opposite sex either. She hadn't wanted to deal with the unwanted teenage pregnancy that her mom had to deal with. She wanted us to have a fresh start without all the temptations of the real world. The sheltering didn't stop there. Every time she got a new husband, she'd give us the usual speech about "inappropriate touches," and although she's getting married, he's still a stranger; then she made us promise to lock the upstairs door at night so no one could get in. None of her husbands were really allowed upstairs, even during the day.

■   ■   ■   ■

It was Friday. We were pulling into a grocery store parking lot in our trusty minivan. A young, white-looking man on a bike waved at us.

"Did you see that?" I whispered to my little brother, pointing.

He hunched his shoulders.

The man parked his bike next to her window. He had the biggest smile on his face. He gave Islamic greetings to her, then looked at us. "Bee-you-ti-fool kids!" he exclaimed in a thick accent and clapped his hands together.

We didn't know what to say back, so Mom said, "Thank you."

As he rode off, Mom twisted her torso to face us in the back seat, and announced, "We're married."

The Algerian dude moved from his small apartment into our two-family flat turned into a one-unit home. No celebration or wedding cake or pretty flower-girl dresses that I desperately yearned for. Mom probably knew deep down inside her troubled heart that just like the others, this union would also not last, so why put up with the fuss of a ceremony.

As his English got better, his temper became worse. Again, she had plucked a dude with the same broken past as hers. His father was also abusive to him and his siblings. He once told us a story, which he rarely ever did. "My brother and I swim in the ocean. A current came and took him. Me, I knew, that if my brother die that day that my father would kill me. So, I jump in." He ended up saving his brother's life at the risk of his own, and we knew that his father hadn't played any games.

Our Algerian stepfather was the type of guy that you couldn't please. Nothing was good enough. Nothing. My brother and I, with Mom, picked out a nice tie from Macy's for Father's Day. We wrapped it and presented it. We were so giddy as he tore the wrapping paper from the box. The excitement on his face drained when he saw the color and pattern. We figured it wasn't his style. He could've pretended to like it, though.

Mom got mad. "You could at least say something!"

They ended up getting into an argument about it. He spat before he stormed out of the side door, "The tie is ugly!"

Needless to say, he never wore that tie.

The last huge fight was the worst.

My half-Algerian baby brother was only about four months old. My other little brother, who had had a growth spurt and was taller than me, was watching cartoons with my little sister upstairs when we heard a *thump* come from downstairs followed by a piercing scream.

It was my infant brother.

We flew down the creaky steps like a herd. Mom was on the floor with her long leg up in the air, trying to kick Algerian stepdaddy away. She didn't have any undies on so her hairy vagina was exposed, as she kicked and kicked and kicked. Next to her was the baby, face down on the carpet, tightly wrapped in a blanket. She'd dropped him during the fight. I rushed over to him. His mouth was wide, his face crimson red, screaming at the top of his lungs. With one hand cradling the infant, my other hand tried to pull back the enraged Algerian. My brother also tried to get in between them to stop the fight.

"Stop it!" Little Sister screamed from the corner, crying.

Somehow, the fight paused, and my mother, siblings, and I took refuge in the classroom where Mom homeschooled us. But the Algerian wouldn't leave. He just paced back and forth, screaming in Arabic, and tossing things over in the living room.

"Get out!" Mom howled.

"I go nowhere," he said through the door. "I pay this house."

Of course, there was no lock on the classroom door. The Algerian tried to get in, and all hell broke loose. He got the door halfway open, and my brother, Little Sis, and I used our bodies to barricade the door. We pushed as he shoved, but he was strong.

The door busted open. I'd never seen my brother, who was thirteen at the time, get so angry before. He was the type of kid who was thoughtful, calm, and good-natured. Fighting and confrontation were against his true self.

He took the Algerian by the collar with both hands and slammed him into the hallway wall. I had had enough. I ran upstairs with the baby and called 911. We had had altercations before, but this one was out of control.

The police came. They allowed the Algerian to pack an overnight bag as he cursed Mom with every step, and then they escorted him out the front door.

He'd lasted about three years. Give or take.

■　■　■　■

In between marriages were the best times. We had just finished a homeschool session, and it was time to play. Little Brother and I grabbed all the pillows and sheets from the beds and closets and started creating forts. We dumped over the toy box and grabbed all the wooden and plastic blocks. The game was called "Block Fight" and was only for true soldiers who could withstand a solid block to the chest or head.

We had just started round one when Mom sent Little Sister upstairs for causing trouble downstairs. We cringed when we heard her Chucky-esque footsteps climbing the steps.

She paused at the door. "I want to play."

I rolled my eyes. "No, you're just gonna get hurt and start crying like a baby like you always do."

"I'm not a baby," she huffed.

"Whatever," I said. "You're not playing."

"Then I'm telling Mom," she countered.

I looked over at Little Brother. He hunched his shoulders. "Fine," I said to her, "but he's on my team."

Happily, she gathered her ammo and fashioned her pile behind the pillow shield.

Little Brother and I were professionals. She didn't stand a chance. We lay on our stomachs and clutched the blocks like grenades. Clearly, she didn't know what she was doing because she sat on her knees, openly exposed. Amateur.

The game had no goal, other than to tear up the body of the opponent. "Aim for her face," I whispered to Little Brother. He nodded like a true soldier.

A barrage of blocks of all shapes and sizes were flung to and fro for about two minutes straight. One block bounced off her forehead. She flinched, but took it like a man. She threw back harder. I got hit in the shoulder. Little Brother got hit in the neck and cheek.

I was down to two colorful wood blocks. I threw one, she ducked, and it missed, hitting the sink behind her.

"Haha." She pointed and jeered.

The last one caught her right in her big eye.

At first, I thought she had fainted by the way she fell down. I rushed from behind the shield and stood over her. No, she wasn't dead. But her face was red, her mouth was wide, and she clutched her eye. Oh no. I looked at Little Brother in horror; she was gearing up for the loudest, most piercing scream of her life. I dropped down to my knees and tried to console her, but it was too late. She shoved my hand away. "I'm. Telling. MOOOOOOOM!"

She jetted down the stairs and into Mom's room. Little Brother and I put our ears to the vent. We were going to get a whuppin'. Period. Mom's heavy footsteps caused the house to shake. She stood at the foot of the stairs and called our names. I took a deep breath, and we took the walk of shame.

With her arms crossed over her chest, Mom stood next to the red-eyed Little Sister. Her pouty lips were tight, and her dark eyes went straight through us. Her foot tapped through her muumuu. "What happened?"

Little Brother, Little Sister, and I spoke over each other, trying to get the first, middle, and last word in.

"Enough," she yelled, holding up her big hand. "Everyone lay down on the floor. On your backs. Now."

We all huffed and moaned simultaneously.

Much more ballsy than the rest, Little Sister whined, "Why?"

Mom gave her "the look." It's hard to explain the full severity of the expression, but it was enough to make us all get down on our hands and knees. Flop on our butts and lay down on our backs. Mom got down on the smooth wooden floor too. Little Sister and Little Brother were too close to one another and bickered.

"Give each other at least an arm's length of space," she instructed.

"Mom, what are we doing?" Little Brother inquired.

"Meditating," Mom answered.

"Meditating?" Little Sister repeated.

"Yes, now close your eyes." Her voice got quieter. "Breathe and listen."

She had closed her eyes, but we hadn't. I kept lifting my head, thinking it was some kind of joke. Why hadn't she just pulled out the belt and whooped us? It would've been faster.

"Close. Your. Eyes!" she bellowed.

I shut them.

"Listen to my voice." She inhaled, then pushed all the air out. "Take a breath in through your nose, real deep, and blow it all out through your mouth until nothing is left."

Little Sister went too fast.

"Slow down," Mom reminded.

"K," she said back.

For a few minutes, we focused on breathing. Although I was getting lightheaded, I felt calmed.

"Now," she said. "I want you to think about one thing. A happy thing. Could be a place. Anything. As long as it's pleasant."

"What about the park?" Little Brother asked.

"Sure."

"Then I'm going to use the park too," Little Sister countered.

"You can't use the park because I'm using the park," he said.

"You guys aren't relaxing your minds," Mom told both of them. "Go to your pleasant place and relax your mind. Relax your body. Breathe in and out, until all the air is gone."

My body was still, as my chest and stomach went up, up, and down. It'd never been so quiet in our house before, not with all the kids running around. Or her exes knocking shit over. I appreciated the sounds of breathing, instead of the usual banter.

Mom kept repeating, *relax your mind and body*, over and over. Until it felt as though my soul had drifted away from my body.

I wish the quiet of that moment had lasted forever. With just us.

■　■　■　■

Mom got married to a butcher from the halal meat store that we visited on the weekends. He was Moroccan and spoke in broken English. He'd always look Mom up and down when she'd walk in to buy her meats in bulk. Then he'd make it a habit to carry all her groceries outside and place them in the back of her car. Such a gentleman. Or so she thought.

She should've known better. He resembled the villain Jafar from *Aladdin*, and that should've been a dead giveaway. He ended up being a heavy drinker and went off on Mom a few times in a drunken rage.

Even though he didn't last, he was around when I got my first period. Awkward, I know. It was even more awkward when he said, "Means you are woman now."

I was ten and a half and playing with my siblings, when my bladder got so full to the point where I couldn't hold it anymore. Almost peeing myself, I pulled down my panties and plopped on the toilet seat. I grabbed a trail of Scott tissue, Mom's fave, and wiped. I looked down as I always did and noticed a streak of pink. I stopped breathing, looking to the left and right of me like I was about to steal candy from the liquor store. Blood? I tossed that tissue in the toilet and wiped again. A do-over. Same colored streak. My coochie was bleeding. Just like Mom's coochie. I had started my period. I'd have to buy those big, thick pads that started at the top of your pelvis and went all the way to the top of your butt crack from the dollar store. How was I going to play with my siblings wearing that shit? And my stomach was going to hurt, and I was going to be mad for no reason at my little play friends next door. I wondered if they had started their periods too. We were all the same age. If they had, I hadn't noticed. They hadn't told me. They probably hadn't. I was weird. An outsider again. I already wore a scarf, and now I had blood coming from my coochie??? And where the fuck was the blood coming from? It was like a gunshot wound I couldn't see. How long was it going to come out? Would I need a blood transfusion? I hadn't even known my blood type.

I stuffed my undies with blobs of tissue and pulled my pants up. No one was to ever find out. The plan was to keep it to myself till I was about seventeen or eighteen. In my mind, that was very doable.

Days passed, and the period was light, so I only had to change the makeshift tissue pad once a day. It wasn't the most comfortable to wear, but I was going to have to get used to it. I had six more years until I could afford real pads. I thought about sneaking into Mom's bathroom and taking one from her stash, but if I kept taking them, she'd notice the count go down for sure. Plus, you couldn't flush the pads like you could the tissue. There couldn't be any evidence.

Mom had an errand to run on the fourth day. I wanted to look fancy, because we were going out. I had a black turtleneck underneath a jacket and a long black skirt with no pants underneath, and my thick-soled emo Mary Janes. I thought I was doing the damn thing. My older sister, Mom, and I stepped onto the elevator and went up to the fourth floor of an office building. We were greeted by a receptionist. Mom went back into one of the private rooms, while me and Big Sis took a seat on the couch and waited.

Between my legs felt squishy as I adjusted myself on the leather couch. I had a bad feeling. Very, very bad. I stood up and surveyed the couch cushion beneath me.

Big Sis frowned. "What are you doing?"

I was trying to see if there was blood on the seat. I gulped. "Nothing. Gotta use the bathroom."

She shrugged and flipped through the pages of a magazine.

I pinched my thighs together and baby-step shuffled toward the receptionist's desk. "Umm, excuse me?"

"Yes?" She glanced over the thin rim of her glasses.

"Where is the bathroom?"

She tilted her head to the left. "Around that hall to your right."

"Thank you." I tightened my butt cheeks, holding what was left of the tissue in place and made the trek.

I grabbed a handful of paper towel and retreated into the nearest stall. To my dismay, whatever was bleeding in my stomach had gone haywire. Blood had soaked through the thin layer of tissue and caused a stain in my white undies. How the hell was Mom going to wash those without seeing the stain? I'd have to bury them under the trash ASAP. Until then, I coated the panties with a thicker and more absorbent paper towel.

When I returned from the bathroom, Mom and Big Sis were standing there, which almost gave me a heart attack.

I clutched my chest. "You guys scared me."

Mom smiled. "Let's go."

They got on the elevator first and I was last. I stepped to the other side and listened to the *ding* with each passing floor.

Mom pointed. "What's that?"

Her long finger pointed to a spot between my shoes. Sitting in plain view was the stack of well-placed paper towels that had once been in my undies, streaked with blood. I bit my bottom lip, eyes darting from her and Big Sis to the pile of nasty napkins taunting me from below. I should've worn leggings under the damn skirt. Before anyone else could see the monstrosity, I trudged over to the napkins, picked them up, and crumbled them in my fist. "It's mine," I admitted.

The last and final ding, and the door slid open.

I found the nearest trash can and pitched my shame. The embarrassment still lingered. It sat on my shoulders during the car ride home and poked at my face like an annoying sibling. Mom looked at me through the rearview mirror. "Amerra, why didn't you tell me you started your period?" *Amerra* is my Muslim name. Means *princess* in Arabic.

I looked out the window and shrugged. "I don't know."

Her jaw tightened, and she gave me the "that-ain't-the-right-answer" look.

"I didn't want you to be mad."

She smiled with those nice, straight white teeth. "Amerra, nothing you do can make me mad."

I smiled back. A bit less guilty.

"A period means you can have kids now."

"Ugggh." I grimaced. "Moooooooom!"

"It's the truth. You're maturing into a woman. Well, your body is, but not your mind just yet. It's a big responsibility."

"I know," I said.

At home, Mom called me downstairs. I raced like a little kid would, skipping every other step. "Yes?"

"You have something waiting for you," she said, and motioned to the top of the mantle above the fireplace.

There sat a medium-sized silver bag. It was very sparkly. Curly strings of ribbon hung from the handle. I knew Big Sis added that touch because Mom wasn't that creative. I slowly walked over to it and brought it down. Inside was a bag of pads, an Archie comic, some chocolate, and a card with a kitten on it. I opened the card, and it had a little message from Mom in it. Something short and sweet.

2. CHILD SUPPORT

Dad is a douche.

He's been one since before I was conceived.

He was the same age as Mom's parents, already older, much older. Knowing him, he probably flashed his thick gold chains and nappy chest hair and new truck, and she spread her legs. But in her defense, she was young, had just come off her second abortion, and was hurting. She thought a man's love would fill the multitude of voids she'd accumulated over the years.

Dad, or what I like to call him, Live Sperm Donor, was from the Deep South, Alabama. He was much shorter than Mom, his friends called him "Red" because he was light-skinned, and his favorite drink was Budweiser. He was a mechanic for General Motors. I believe he test-drove cars. Cars were his life. He even had a side gig of fixing cars out of his garage. His hands stayed caked in motor oil, and he wore a weathered baseball cap, which covered his smooth, bald head, and a toothpick that'd poke out of the corner of his mouth. He spoke real fast and real country and had a bad stutter. He was never broke though, even though he always claimed he was.

He was secretive about his life, too, never really divulging the details of his past. One time, I had begged to come over for the weekend; I didn't want to be around Mom. Usually, he'd lie and say he'd pick me up but would never come. But that weekend, he finally drove the thirty minutes and got me, and I was excited just to be around him.

Morning came. I was eating a bowl of Corn Pops. He opened the side door and asked me to help him in the garage. I quickly finished and rinsed my bowl and slid into a pair of scuffed gym shoes.

In his garage, his sanctuary, he asked me to hold up the light, so he could dig deeper into the engine. I held the lamp close and steady as he tightened bolts. We worked in silence. He wasn't much of a talker. Not to us kids anyway.

His wife, my stepmother, was taking us to the movies later when she got off work. It was the perfect opportunity to ask for a few bucks for snacks.

"Dad?"

"Yeah?" He rustled about in his toolbox.

"We're going to the movies . . ." I paused, not knowing if he was listening or not. I waited for confirmation.

"Yeah?"

"I was thinking that maybe you could give me a few dollars?" I cringed inside. He always made me feel uncomfortable when I spoke around him or asked him for anything.

He readjusted my hand so that the lamp would shine exactly where he wanted it. After hammering a part of the engine, he said, "We use' to pick cotton in Alabama. Fingers would be to'e up. Use' to work hard out in the hot sun."

I took that statement as, the current youth thought that their parents were made out of money and that I wasn't getting a penny.

Later on, he left $20 with my stepmom.

The second thing he told me about his past was on one occasion on our way back to Mom's house. Dad always kept top-of-the-line vans. Fully loaded with two mini-televisions, leather seats, and decorative lights on the ceiling. I'd never been inside a fancy vehicle before, so I enjoyed riding with him.

I'm not sure how or why he divulged what he had, but he told me that his father was very mean and never gave them money. I remember my twelve-year-old self feeling bad for him, but it put a lot into perspective.

Although I knew nothing about him, I still fantasized about who he *could* be. I'd heard stories about him always picking me up when I was a baby. Showing me off next to his bright yellow Corvette. Being that kind of dad, the one a daughter could be proud of. Then something happened. I'm not sure what that something was. Perhaps it was Mom, or maybe it was child support, or maybe as time went on, he'd just forgotten about me too easily. Still, I always chose him over Mom, even when he never did the same for me. I was the last pick in his world. I was young; I didn't care and gave him chance after chance. I needed a daddy so bad that I was willing to take anything. Mom's fly-by-night husbands were watered-down versions of him. I needed something tangible.

Wanting to know more about Dad, I asked Mom to tell me more about him. Mom had an odd sense of humor. "When I was pregnant with you, we had got into an argument about something. I picked up the phone while he was still talking. I didn't care, as far as I was concerned the conversation was over. He asked me to put the phone down, and I refused. He took the phone from me and tapped me on the forehead. I snatched it back. A few seconds later, blood poured down my face. He had torn the skin. He started freaking out and trying to stop the bleeding. You know, I have sensitive skin."

Mom and Dad would have their monthly phone battles, usually regarding me. For the most part, it was about child support. Him lying about picking me up when he had no intention of doing so. Him sneaking pork into my meals knowing full well that I was Muslim. Him trying to still solicit Mom for sex, even though he was married to Stepmom. There would have been even more battles and maybe violence, if I'd told Mom that he'd emotionally abuse me when she wasn't around.

He'd make comments about my weight. A lot. I was a chubby, Muslim kid who was odd and liked fantasy novels. He'd make snarky comments about my hijab and not being able to wear shorts and Mom homeschooling me.

One time, I was in the kitchen making breakfast with my twin step-siblings. Mom had bought me this Bill Cosby sweater that I picked out. She barely allowed me to pick out my own clothes. It was big, but I liked it. Dad stood over the stove, making bacon. Stepmom was pouring herself a cup of coffee.

"You want some?" he asked me.

One of the twins shouted, "Bacon is so good!"

"No, thanks," I said. He knew I couldn't eat bacon.

He grumbled, "That's cuz ya' crazy mama and that Izlam. Ain't nuthin' wrong with bacon."

Dad also had a bad temper. Because he was angry that I said no to bacon, he called Mom and started going off. He called her crazy because she was Muslim. He told her that the "Moozlum" food she was feeding me was making me fat. He told her that I should be in public school like the rest of the kids. He called her crazy a few more times, then hung up on her.

Stepmom. The twins. We all sat silent.

Then he turned his anger to me, pointing the greasy spatula at my sweater. "Why she put you in these big, ugly clothes? I gave her money to buy you something else."

I shrank to the size of a mouse as he continued his attack. Stepmom finally stepped in and said that was enough.

He scoffed, chewed on his bacon, and left.

Later on, Stepmom pulled me aside. "You know how your dad is. Personally, I think your sweater is cute."

"Thank you," I said. Mom always told me to be polite.

■ ■ ■ ■

We were poor growing up. Child support was spotty to nonexistent. Mom and her family weren't on speaking terms because of their inability to accept Mom's religion as well as her craziness.

So, it was all on her to provide. Some things she did were illegal, and other times she'd create her own opportunities, like she started a neighborhood childcare from her home. And of course, we relied on that good old government welfare.

The lights got cut off once, and one time, we only had beans and cornbread to eat for dinner for a few weeks. We had the minimum, but what we had was enough. TV was a huge staple in the house. My siblings and I got to explore the world and live vicariously through white characters. Shows like *Saved by the Bell* and *Blossom* and *Sabrina the Teenage Witch* showed me that the closer my Black skin was to their whiteness, I could be that quirky lead with a few bumps during the day, but by the end of the episode, everything would be alright. But that wasn't my world at all. At the end of the episode, I still lived in the real world. The world of a child of color living in the ghetto. Unable to scrub off her melanin, no matter how hard she tried, no matter how many episodes she'd studied and finished. She'd never be like those child actors who had two biological parents and real beds with matching comforter sets. Her reality was mattresses on the floor, strange men whom she wanted so badly to be her real daddy that came and went, but mostly went. Those characters became an obsession for me. A getaway from my own little child life. If only for just thirty minutes.

Commercials were the best though. We would choose our favorite ones and learn all the lines so that when they came on, we could repeat along.

One was the Cedar Point commercial. Man, they had the water parks and roller coasters. And we figured out that it was in Sandusky, Ohio, only about three hours away. We raced to the computer and signed into AOL. We waited patiently as the running man emoji connected to the internet. We searched admission prices. They were a bit high, but not like Disneyland prices. So, it was a possibility that one day Mom would take us. The trip became our yearly dream.

Year after year passed, and Mom still didn't have enough money to take us. As a kid, I got it. But it didn't hurt any less. I'd take the Cedar Point advertisements from the mail up to my room and read them over and over, imagining myself strapped into the Midwest's tallest coaster and just flying. In my vision, I also had long, blonde hair that flapped in the wind.

It was early in the day, Mom was on the phone in the kitchen, dragging the long cord to and fro as she paced. By her stern tone, I knew it was someone's daddy on the other end.

I listened quietly by the steps. "You never take her anywhere! She has a right to travel with you to Cedar Point, just as those other kids you claim do. She's *your* daughter."

It was my dad on the other end.

■   ■   ■

Spring had arrived. Spring in Michigan was magical. Red and blue birds chirped. Wild flowers sprang to life, and the trees were lush and full. The air even smelled different. New.

"Your dad's outside," one of my siblings told me.

I rushed around the corner, burst out the door, and hopped over four cement steps, landing on the sidewalk. I looped around the front yard and noticed Mom and him talking. I stood by the side of the old station wagon and waited for the adults to finish their conversation. Mom's arms were crossed over her chest and her lips were pursed. I couldn't see his expression, just the back of his head.

"Why can't she go to Cedar Point with you? She'd really enjoy that. Take her."

And with conviction he replied, "She can't go."

"Why not?"

"Because that scarf on her head might get stuck in the rides," he continued. "And she can't wear shorts. It's gonna be hot."

Mom's mouth drooped. She was saddened by his idiotic attempt to justify such foolishness. "She's over there." Mom opened the side door. It creaked, then slammed behind her.

He approached. Eyes squinting against the sun. That same old toothpick dangling from the edge of his lips. He hugged me. I hugged back.

Repeating what he said again stung worse. "That thing on your head would get stuck in the coaster. You know that, right?"

"Dad, it won't. I promise," I pleaded. "I can tie it in the back. See." I demonstrated, tying it very tight.

"We'll see," he said. "Go'n on and get ya mama."

When a Black parent said, "We'll see," it usually meant a definite no.

I was nine years old and nowhere close to getting to Cedar Point.

It wasn't until I was thirteen when he finally decided that I was worthy enough to take a trip to Cedar Point with him and his family. I wasn't sure if he felt guilted into doing it or he was being genuine in his attempt to reconnect, but I saw his bad patterns a little differently than when I was smaller. Resentment had started to form toward him. The first streaks of hatred materialized.

The sun followed us throughout the park. No cloud in sight. I got the worst tan ever that day. But I'd finally made it to my childhood dream park. For that, I was grateful. Dad and his wife didn't want to ride the roller coasters, and they had my little sister with them, so we all just split up. I went with the twins. Man, we tore up that park. Cracking jokes. Laughing. Standing in those long-ass lines. We rode the first coaster. We held our hands high in the air as we were propelled along a winding track. Our necks whipped and our legs dangled. The fat in our cheeks jiggled as the wind slapped us. My heart thumped, fear and exhilaration mixed into one.

My scarf hadn't fallen off either. Not once. It hadn't got caught in the tracks, derailed the seats, and killed everyone, like Dad had initially feared.

The ride came to a complete stop.

"Yooooooo," one of the twins breathed hard. "I'm over here cryin'."

Tears rolled from her eyes. We burst out laughing and pushed each other playfully.

Our fun time had elapsed, and it was time to meet back with Dad.

We found them at some kiddy ride, watching my little sister ride the pink elephant around in a circle.

"Y'all hungry?" Dad asked.

All three of us bobbed our heads.

He pulled out a park pamphlet and searched for eateries nearby.

"This burger place sounds good." He pointed.

My anxiety intensified. Dad hated when I brought my religion into anything, but I couldn't eat the hamburgers. I couldn't ask if they had vegetarian options either because there was a chance that he'd still flip out and regret bringing me. So, I walked with them, the addition to the family who couldn't just be like them. Eat like them. Show my hair like them. Be Christian like them.

Dad opened the door for everyone, but before I stepped inside, I paused.

"You know what, there's this really cool game that I saw on the way here," I lied. "I'm actually not even hungry."

He didn't ask questions. He pulled out a twenty-dollar bill and handed it to me. "Be back here in an hour." He disappeared into the burger joint.

I walked away. Alone, I checked out the game row. Stuffed animals hung from the booths. Lights flashed and hosts called out over the loud speaker to people passing, challenging them to hit the jackpot. Instead of feeling sorry for myself, I decided to play a game. The one where you have to toss the ping-pong ball into small cups. I played once and lost. I played again. And lo and behold, I won! The bells whistled, and the host told me that I could pick out one big stuffed animal. I chose a Pokémon character. A few watchers patted me on my back and gave me high-fives. I had never won anything in my life. I felt special for once.

Still hungry and only with ten bucks left, I grabbed an elephant ear and drank water from the fountain. I took a seat on a bench, sat my new stuffed friend down, and munched on the sugary fried goodness. I people-watched. That was fun. Watching the families go back and forth.

It was time to go back to Dad and his family. I entered the restaurant and saw them at a nearby booth. It only had enough room for the five of them. Even if I had been able to eat the burgers and fries, there would have been nowhere for me to sit. He probably would've made me sit at another table or something.

One of the twins pointed at my prize. "Whoa, you hit the jackpot."

"I know." I smiled, lifting the animal higher.

Stepmom pulled out her throwaway camera. "Let's all take a picture." She searched around for someone to take it, but all the waitresses were busy bussing tables.

I held my hand out. "I'll take it."

She appeared hesitant. Like she wanted me to be in the photo. Finally, she gave it to me.

Dad never got up and offered to take his daughter's place. Instead he posed, and I took a picture of him and his lovely family at Cedar Point.

3. VERNON V. SMILEY

Because I was homeschooled, I'd never stepped foot in a public or private school. Many people thought it was weird that a single, Black mother was homeschooling all of her children. It was definitely odd to see people's expressions change when she divulged that bit of info. The follow-up question was always the same: well, then, how are they gonna learn how to socialize with other children? Mom would always reply with a hidden annoyance, "My kids are very social."

As a child, I'd just avoided the topic altogether because kids would always make fun of me when I told them that I had never been to an actual school.

"Your mom is the teacher?" One neighborhood girl asked in a group of her friends.

"Yep," I nodded. "We have a classroom and everything."

Her lips pursed as she pretended to think really hard. "So, ummm, how do parent-teacher conferences work?" And everyone had a good laugh except me.

I begged my mom to let me go to real school after that. Mostly because I needed to go to prom like the other girls and not be made fun of for being different, but I told her I needed to go for the scholarships and other academic opportunities since she was heavy into her kids receiving the best education. Instead, she'd always say that we'd look into it next year, but years past, and I still wasn't enrolled. I took that as a hard no and set my sights on living my real adult life in college.

The idea of school, higher education, was always attractive to me. Most likely because of film and TV. You could be anyone you wanted in college. You could create your own narrative. Be your own boss. And boys, lots of boys with no parental supervision. I didn't want to be that shy Muslim girl who spent a lot of her time reading sci-fi novels at the local library anymore. I wanted to be seen as a serious adult, ambitious, going somewhere in life.

To me, college meant being my own person. Legal independence from Mom. Plus, there wasn't any other options. It was either go to school or get married and have kids. It seems so black and white now, but those are all the choices I thought I had. And I damn sure wasn't getting married or having kids like a lot of other young Muslim girls my age. I wasn't about to escape one ruling to go live under another.

I had no idea how much college cost or about living on my own, but I just knew that I had to go.

Mom had three kids under me, so I didn't expect her to pay for college. I was on my own. I thought about stripping like the white girls, because I had watched some reality shows about how poor girls pay for college and that seemed to be the most popular thing to do, but I was fat and had joint issues and a weak upper body. It'd take a miracle from God to get me to the top of that shiny pole. Working full-time was an option, but then I'd have to cut my credit hours in half. Also, I didn't plan on being in school for six years like my older sister. I was too eager to start my life as a graduate.

I filled out the FASFA with Mom's help. I got enough funds to cover most of the tuition but not books and the other fees.

Mom noticed my frustration. "I'll look through my paperwork, but there's a little state stipend you can get since we've been on food stamps for a while. And I believe that your father, through his job, can get you a grant as well. Call him."

I shuddered. I was at that age where I no longer idolized him or what he could be. I knew who he was, because he'd shown me time after time that he was never to be trusted. And frankly, I was disgusted by his inability to just be there. Unfortunately, he was too busy making kids around the Midwest and South behind my stepmother's back to care about his daughter graduating and wanting to further her education. So that was that.

Months passed, and we'd been receiving regular child support payments. I was excited that Mom put half of each check in a savings account for a car. I was working part-time at a doughnut shop making $7.15 per hour, but I needed a lot more.

"Did you call your father about the grant?" she reminded me.

"No. Not yet." I frowned.

"Amerra, call your father."

I figured he couldn't still be that mad at us for the whole child support thing. And I really needed the money for school. The worst he could say was no.

I called. As the phone rang, my stomach churned. I dreamed for the voicemail to just pick up so I could leave a message.

It rang like five times.

Instead of the pleasant voicemail lady picking up, it was him. "Hella?" Despite living in Michigan for many decades, he still had a deep Southern accent.

I rolled my eyes. "Heeeeeey, D-dad!"

"Wassup?"

"Actually, I was calling because Mom said you had some information for me about that school program GM offers . . ."

He had really bad allergies and went into a coughing, sniffling, and sneezing fit. "Ugh. Go to this website. All the information is on there."

"Oh, okay. Thanks."

"Yup." Then he hung up.

The grant turned out to be a tuition reimbursement program, which meant I had to put up the money first. By then, I was in my third semester, so I applied for the reimbursement of the previous two semesters. One of the things they needed on the application was Dad's Social Security number and birth date. I didn't have those bits of information, so I dialed him. "Dad, remember that program I told you about? Well, they need some of your information in order to process it."

"What are they asking for?" He was out of breath, probably with his head deep under the hood of a car.

"They want your soc and birth date," I explained.

He paused, then said, "You don't know my birthday?"

"Dad, no, I—"

"Have your mama call me."

Click.

Mom called him. He gave her trouble too. Obviously, he hadn't wanted to help me get reimbursed after all. But why bring it up? Why tell Mom about the program in the first place, just to snatch it away at the last moment? At the end of the call, he hadn't given her anything more than he'd given me. I officially hated him. I thought he was the devil reincarnated. And I was the spawn. I didn't have a chance.

"Well." Mom pursed her lips together. "There may be some of his info on those child support papers. Worth a look."

A huge smile crawled across my face. There was still hope.

We ended up locating the files, and lo and behold, in the top right corner was his information.

I entered his numbers into the missing fields of the application and clicked submit.

"Thanks, Mom." I looked at her over my shoulder.

"No problem, baby."

Eight weeks passed and still no reimbursement check. I was well into my fourth semester and banking on that money to cover bills. I had called a few weeks earlier to see if I needed to send any more paperwork, but the lady assured me that it was completed, and the funds were on their way.

Another week passed and still no check. Maybe they got my address mixed up with Dad's. I called again and asked them what address they had on file. They told me they had his and that it'd be sent to his address. Weird, but whatever. I'd just let him know the deal and all would be good with life.

"For some reason, my school money will be sent to your house. If you can keep a lookout for me that'd be great," I told him over the phone.

"Yup," he said.

Maybe he wasn't as bad as I thought after all.

Two weeks had come and gone, and I hadn't received a call. I knew it should've been there by now. I called him twice, inquiring about the mail. Both times, he'd said he'd received nothing. I waited a few days and decided to make a trip all the way to Southfield with my janky car—it had bad brakes and five bucks in the tank—to search through his mail. He had to have just overlooked it. He was the same age as my grandparents and probably getting more and more senile as the days passed. He must've overlooked it. He just had to.

I pulled up his gravel driveway with my silver Hyundai Accent. It was on its last leg and Dad refused to fix it, always claiming that he was too busy. So, I was forced to go to underground mechanics who were just messing it up even more. The car drove solely on a wish and a prayer.

Dad's face popped up from behind a car. He never smiled when he saw me, just kept that same resting bitch face as if I was bothering his very existence. I got out and walked to him.

"Wassup?"

"Nothing much." I dug the tip of the boot into the pebbles. "I called the lady and she said that check was sent out already. Weeks ago. Can I go check through your mail to see if you maybe overlooked it?"

He wiped his greasy hands on an even greasier, oil-stained towel. "I ain't overlook nothin', but go'on 'head."

I jogged up the stairs and searched through their little pile of mail on top of the microwave. I checked twice. To my dismay, it wasn't there. I sulked down the stairs and back outside.

"Find it?" he asked.

"Nah," I said. "I'll check again next week."

I got in my loud-ass car and drove off.

I finally called the office again. There must've been a mix-up with the addresses or some glitch in the system.

"My name is Leah Vernon and I'm calling about the status of my reimbursement check."

She typed in my name and account number. "Says here that it was mailed out about six weeks ago and was cashed."

My body stiffened. "What? That's not possible. I didn't get anything, and I certainly never cashed that check."

More typing. "Says that the check was cut to the employee and that the funds have been deposited."

"Th-that's my dad." My chest hurt as it constricted around my lungs, making it difficult to breathe.

"He is the employee, correct?"

"Y-yes."

"The checks are always cut to the employee."

"But it's my money," I pleaded. "I'm the one who paid for my schooling, not him. He just stole my money! He took my money for school. What kind of douche bag takes money from his own struggling daughter?"

"Ma'am, seems like you need to speak with him."

I tightened my eyes, trying to trap the tears. "I'm sorry. Thank you."

I'd never in my life thought that another human being could be so low. So low that they were beneath dirt and shit. I also never thought that I could hate someone as much as I hated him. I was young and broke and full of angst. I was fat, Black, Muslim, and poor. I watched my white classmates take the summers off and go to Italy and China, as I busted my ass to stay afloat in school, taking fuckin' fifteen credits at a time so that I could graduate early. So that I could get a job, take care of myself, be a nice fuckin' upstanding American citizen! And he had the audacity to steal—not take, not borrow—*steal* over two thousand dollars from me? He had a nice home, several nice cars. He had a wife who worked. He had an amazing job and a side hustle. He was living the life. I, on the other hand, could barely afford toothpaste and tampons.

He stole. From me. He lied. To me. He made me think for months that my money had gone missing, that there was a mistake or it was the department's fault. He made me waste gas. He made me believe that he wasn't as evil as I initially thought. That maybe he had a heart somewhere deep in the blackness of his chest.

I got conned by my own father.

And because of that, I became hardened.

I was out for blood.

■ ■ ■ ■

"I'm suing him," I told Mom. "He stole it. Every penny."

She lowered her head in disgrace, then said, "Do what you have to do."

I researched on Ask Jeeves how to sue someone, because Google wasn't a thing at that time. It was a small-claims matter, which meant I had to go through the magistrate in his city. I filed the complaint. Gave the lady all his information. She smiled and stamped "received" on the application. She told me to have a nice day.

He kept trying stupid antics to postpone the hearing. He successfully delayed it twice. The third time, she told him that it couldn't be delayed any longer and if he didn't show up, then they'd rule in my favor. Case closed.

I sat in the second row waiting for our case to be called: *Vernon v. Smiley*. I was scared and alone. I'm not sure why I hadn't asked anyone to go with me. My leg jiggled nervously as I intertwined my fingers on my thigh. A folder with old receipts and the application I initially submitted sat on the empty seat next to me.

In my peripheral vision, I saw him walk in the door. I stared. He stared, then looked away and took a seat. No hi, hello, or wave.

"*Vernon v. Smiley*," the mediator called from an open door.

I stood, collected my things, and entered the dark room. It had a huge round table. She sat at the head, and Dad and I sat across from each other. It was so matter-of-fact, like we were just two people who'd never met. She explained the process. She said that if we couldn't come to a conclusion then and there, that it'd go in front of a judge.

"So, what do y'all want to do?" She eyed us both.

Dad scooted his chair close to the edge of the table and set his elbows on the shiny, flat surface. His face was yellow, with wrinkles on the forehead and at the edges of his eyes. He never smiled. Two of his buttons near his neck were unbuttoned. He opened his mouth to expose two gold teeth. He had a stuttering problem because he spoke so fast. "I'll g-g-give her the money."

"Good," the mediator said. "When will you be able to cut her a check?"

"Couple weeks."

"Alright, so you have thirty days to give Ms. Vernon $2,198." She scribbled on a form, then handed it to me to sign first.

"I'm t-t-taking you out of my will, and you're no longer my daughter," he told me.

The mediator held her chest. "Oh."

I looked up at him, pen still in hand, and smiled. I'm sure I looked like the Joker. "I never *was* your daughter, George."

PART 2
JEZEBEL

▪ ▪ ▪ ▪ ▪ ▪ ▪ ▪ ▪

4. FLUSHED

"I know this from experience: don't lose your virginity to someone you like," my friend cautioned like a ghetto shaman, placing three generic condoms she'd gotten for free from Planned Parenthood in the middle of my palm. "Take these. You might need 'em one day."

I wasn't going to need them, I thought. Mom taught me better than that. I was a good girl. I wasn't like her, in the streets, hopping from dick to dick. I was waiting until marriage, like the good book ordered. I wanted to go to heaven, and if keeping my legs closed got me there, then that was the least I could do. I was the only girl in the group who hadn't lost her virginity yet. I hadn't even done so much as make out with a boy. I hadn't touched liquor or weed at parties. I fasted during Ramadan and prayed every Friday at the mosque. I wore my hijab with pride. I was untainted and untouched. And I took pride in that, knowing that I was purer than the rest. Better than them. Stronger than them.

How weak they were to not listen to God.

∎ ∎ ∎ ∎

An Aquarius, he was more observant than talkative. Sensitive and naïve and calm. A sense of humor and an odd laugh. He had one dimple on his left cheek and a pointy nose that used to poke out of a huge black hoodie he thought was so cool. He played basketball and football at an inner-city school. Grew up in a bad neighborhood but had both parents. His family was dysfunctional, but they tried hard to hide it and save face for the Islamic community they lived in.

I, on the other hand, came from a single-family household. Mom was married more times than I can remember. I was hardheaded, a dreamer, and a go-getter. I didn't trust people.

I trusted him, though. He wasn't like the douche bags Mom brought home.

He was different.

My life was sporadic.

Mom was trying to control me, keep me in her dream world like she had her husbands. But I was slipping away into adulthood. Out of her jurisdiction. I was struggling in college. A homeschooled Black girl from Detroit with too many issues to name. The odds were already stacked two miles high. My debit card had just been declined. Lack of sufficient funds. Unlike my other classmates, I had no parents to send me some much-needed cash.

We were young when we met. I had just come out of a secret long-distance relationship with a young man who'd joined the Marines. We were obsessed with one another. He'd somehow rig a phone out in the desert of Iraq, and the number would pop up on my end with about twenty random numbers. We'd talk late into the night, then into the wee hours of the morning. Although he wasn't Muslim, I had planned on running away to California to be with him.

Mom found out about our fling when he sent me a bouquet of flowers to the house. She didn't freak like I thought she would, but I was nervous nonetheless.

When he came back home from tour, shit got real. I concocted some imaginary story about him cheating on me with an old girlfriend, when what I was really doing was digging for a break-up justification because he wasn't Muslim. And I couldn't be with a non-Muslim man.

I was better than that.

It was that summer that I met this Muslim boy. I knocked on his family's door. He answered. When he saw me, he seemed shy. Being the attitude-ridden, hormonal teen that I was, and assuming he was way younger than me, I rolled my eyes and asked if his sister was there. He nodded, then ran halfway up the stairs to alert his sister to my arrival.

"Umm, you can go up." He looked down at his feet bashfully, avoiding eye contact.

"Ooookay," I replied, elongating the "O" sound. He must've been the annoying little brother.

As I tried to pass him on the steps, he wouldn't move. I ended up having to squeeze past him, and my hips brushed up against him.

He smiled wide.

I grimaced.

"Is your brother weird or something?" I asked his sister.

"No!" she yelled. "He probably just likes you."

"Eww, he's ugly," I scoffed.

"My brother is not ugly."

"Sure."

After weeks of my friends telling me how much he liked me, I gave up and went out on a double-date with him and some mutual friends.

Our first kiss was the sweetest thing. We were at an empty park at night. His nose brushed past my cheek. We kind of stayed stationary for a while, neither one of us wanting to make the first move. At some point, our lips met. He wasn't that ugly, annoying kid I thought he was only weeks ago. He wasn't ugly at all, but the most beautiful person I'd known.

He and I would hang out in vacant parking lots in the hood and make out. He'd grab my booty, and our tongues would thrash madly with adolescent passion.

One chilly morning, we drove around until three in the morning. "Let's go to your place," I said.

He shook his head. "My sisters are home tonight. Babysitting."

"Oh," I huffed. I didn't want our time together to end. Plus, I couldn't go back home because it was super late. I wasn't in the mood to hear Mom's mouth.

"Well, if you want, we could go half-half on a room?" I suggested.

He sniffed. "Yeah. We can do that."

Motel 6 was down the street. We pulled up into the lot, then entered the lobby like two little shits. The once white tiling was a dingy eggshell color. An off-brand pop machine stood across from two attached waiting-room chairs. A door that read "Employees Only" faced us, and next to that was a thick plate-glass window. Behind that, sitting on a stool watching television, was a Black woman with a weave bun on top of her head.

"How much?" he asked her.

Sixty-four ninety-nine, plus tax." The girl wouldn't take her eyes from the old movie. "IDs," she said.

He looked at me for approval. I nodded.

We placed our cards under the barrier that protected the worker from late-night crazies.

She finally looked at us, narrowing her wide-set eyes. Her fat lips were pursed as she attempted to match our faces to the bad state ID photos. "You gotta' be twenty-one to rent here." She flung them back under the glass and went back to watching the flick.

Another motel was not too far down the road and off the freeway. Super shady, but not the shadiest. He went into the lobby for about ten minutes. My stomach was queasy; things were jumping around.

He returned to the car with two door keys.

Reality hit.

The room smelled like old cigarettes and mothballs. Usually, I'd have complained, but I was silent. The door shut. I jumped, surprised at how hard it slammed. It had to have woken up the prostitutes and pimps residing in the next couple of rooms. He locked the bottom lock, then slid the top chain through its track.

We were alone.

He took off his shoes, hoodie, then pants, and slipped under the blankets. I removed my shoes, then turned the TV on. I sat at the edge of the bed.

"Want me to turn off the lights?" he asked.

I shook my head. "I got it."

The volume was low. Fast-paced clips of the item they were selling flashed in quick bursts. Bright-colored boxes reading "buy now" and "while quantities last" blinked. A 1-800 number in bold was stamped at the bottom.

"Act now," the presenter said and pointed at me. "Before it's too late!"

Only the glare from an infomercial illuminated his brown face when I looked back at him. He took my arm and pulled me in. He wanted something from me. Like the other men. Just like Mom said.

Looking me up and down, he laughed. "Why do you have all those clothes on?"

I shrugged. "I don't know. Cold."

"Well, let me warm you up," he said. "Body heat transfers better with skin-to-skin contact."

He lifted my shirt over my head, careful not to pull off my scarf. Instead of letting it hang in front, I tied it like a turban, wanting to maintain some sort of modesty. He unbuckled my pants next. I lay on my back, and he slid them down over my knees, then to my ankles. One leg at a time, those came completely off too. The only flimsy protection I had left were cotton undies and a sports bra from Walmart.

I thought that maybe I'd be more self-conscious of my fat body sitting there half-naked, since I'd never actually been naked in front of a boy before, other than my little brothers. But my deep-rooted insecurities seemed to be nonexistent as I geared up for much more important decisions.

I was totally out of my good-girl element. Mom tried to give us the very uncomfortable sex talk, and we'd just drown her out with "oohs" and "aahs." She'd give us books on female and male genitalia and STDs. I knew all about AIDS and genital warts. But nothing about the actual thing. I mean, I watched a few blurry soft pornos when the TV would pick up HBO, but that's as far as my knowledge went.

He hugged me. It felt foreign but right. The fine hairs on the back of my neck stood upright as he dug his face into my neck.

All of my silent worries drifted away like smoke.

A hug turned into a kiss. Then a kiss turned into neck bites. Dry humping. My bra came off.

"Let me put the tip in," he said breathlessly into my ear.

"No," I exclaimed, pushing him away but not protesting.

"Come on, just the tip," he said. "I want you."

He kissed me again, this time with tongue, as I pressed my body into his. I bit his lip. He pinned me down and kissed all the way down my chest and stopped at my nipple. When his teeth glided over my areola, I lost my shit.

Complete control dissolved.

"Fine, but you've gotta wear a condom," I told him.

He reached into his wallet on the shoddy nightstand and pulled out a Magnum.

I was a fat girl, not as fat as I am now, but still fat. He kept missing my vagina and trying to stick it in the flap of my FUPA. After a few failed attempts to locate the X, I gently led the way.

He didn't make it all the way in before he came. He tried to pretend he hadn't, but instantly became flaccid. I didn't feel anything.

Without exaggeration, the entire ordeal was three minutes, tops. Questions and concerns flooded my mind: I don't think he did it right. Was that how it always happened? Was that very short three minutes the three minutes of my life that bought me a one-way ticket to Muslim girl hell? Without an apology or explanation, he rolled over. He must've been gearing up for round two, I thought. That first round was a practice try obviously. He'd lay the real sex on me shortly. So, I waited, face up and underneath the itchy blankets. Waiting for him to roll back over.

Soft snoring. His chest peacefully rose and fell, as I lay there in utter confusion, afraid to move. I was afraid to move from that spot, because once I got out of that bed and returned to the real world, the grave mistake that I'd made would be solidified.

My first time was supposed to be special. I was supposed to be married. In my diary, the one with the mini heart-shaped lock and key, I had the whole thing planned out. Find a tall, dark-skinned, handsome fellow who believed in Allah and had a nice car, deep dimples, and some cash. He was going to get down on one knee in the most romantic way. Maybe something cliché like in front of the Eiffel Tower. Everyone would be so jealous that I'd snagged a dude without using my vagina to seduce him. That he was just as holy as I was and also waited to have sex. Our wedding would be grand. Over the top. Because, of course, God would favor us and give us lots of funds because we were his most faithful servants. Then I'd be all shy on the honeymoon, and then he'd kiss my cheek ever so softly, then guide me underneath the bed's canopy and take my virginity.

And it'd last way more than three minutes.

I was a stone. My reality was that I just lost my virginity in a motel off I-696. No canopy. No grand scheme. It was as simple as simple could get. I was embarrassed and regretful that I'd just tossed my religion away for that. Three. Fuckin'. Minutes!

Sleep continued to evade me as I desperately begged for it to take me out of my misery. His soft snore. The haunting whir of the air conditioner. My own thoughts of indecency. All those factors kept me wide awake.

For a while, I strategized about what would be the best thing to do at that moment. Some thoughts ranged from just lying there until the sun came up and check out, pretending nothing was wrong, like a normal person. Another was just beating his ass awake and screaming about how he just ruined my chances of ever making it to paradise.

The last was just leaving him there. Driving far, far away and never looking back. Just forgetting about the whole thing and pretending it never, ever happened. Maybe if I kept my legs closed and became the equivalent of an Islamic nun, then maybe God would find it in his ethereal heart to forgive me.

I couldn't make a decision on what to do, but I knew that I had to get out of there. I finally put my clothes back on and stood by the door. I flicked on the lights and cleared my throat.

One of his eyes squinted open. "What's going on?"

I pointed to the clock. "I'm ready to go."

The car ride back home was quiet. I didn't talk to him for weeks after what I referred to as "the incident."

■ ■ ■ ■

The thing about being young and hormonal and hot and ready and suppressed all the time is that once you get a taste of something forbidden, you just keep going back, no matter how bad it is for you.

My anger about "the incident" dissolved, and I met up with him a few times over the next couple of weeks. I'd sneak into his parents' place late at night, but we wouldn't do anything like that last time. Early one morning, his sisters were all asleep, and I wiggled through the side door and darted to his room. We ate cold BBQ chicken and watched old VHS tapes. We started making out again once the lights were out. He suggested I get on top. This time he did it right. I felt all of it—every uncomfortable poke—and though painful at times, I liked it.

"Relax," he whispered after he flipped me on my back.

How could I relax? I was losing my virginity—for the second time—to a Muslim boy that I wasn't married to. I was going to be dubbed a bona fide ho if my indecencies were discovered. And if Mom found out, she'd drop-kick me. Or worse, disown me or maybe murder me!

The cherry was popped that time. The deed was done. He asked if I was okay. I was not, but said I was. I didn't want to talk about it.

I felt even worse than the first time, like I'd betrayed someone. Something. God was looking at me. And he wasn't pleased. I knew it.

The next morning, I felt like shit. An agonizing period that no one bothered to tell me about once you lose your virginity. I wore a hoodie all day and stayed locked up in my room. I could've sworn Mom knew what I'd done. God probably told her. Had that shit on tape and played it for her. Jezebel was stamped on my forehead. I pulled the hoodie down a little more to cover my face.

"Everything alright?" she asked when I came down for a meal. She knew something.

I nodded vigorously. "Everything's great."

I was so ashamed; I stopped returning his texts.

Several weeks passed before he finally called. "What's up?" he asked.

"Nothin'," I said.

"Oh." Pause. "You mad at me or something?"

"Nope."

After a joke, he never waited for people to process it and laugh. He'd always laugh before the punchline was done. He made one then. I don't remember exactly what he said, but I know it made me smile. He was always able to make me smile or chuckle when I hadn't wanted to but when I needed to. I had always been so serious and guarded. It was as if he was the balance that I was missing.

We were back cool again. And he was there for me, as I transitioned from teenhood to adulthood. We'd cuddle and watch movies. And have sex. So much sex. His parents were getting suspicious because of his big-mouthed siblings. His father told him it was wrong for a Muslim to fornicate, that he knew better, but he'd just lie and say that he wasn't doing anything.

Then I started to feel bad. Mom wasn't hovering over me telling me that I was a bad girl, but I knew the rules. And I was breaking them.

On one particular night, I lay beside him on a futon mattress and cried, silently. He pulled me close and wiped my tears away. "What's wrong?"

I pulled the blanket up to cover myself. I felt nasty and exposed. "What we're doing is wrong. It's not right."

He kissed my forehead. "I know."

The push of sexual desire versus the pull of religion took its toll. I'd have nights where I'd cry because I felt disgusting. He'd cry, too, because his father wanted him to be a good Muslim man. And together, we were failing miserably.

But we chose not to stop, and things only got worse.

We always used condoms, but one time it broke without my knowledge.

Out of breath, I said, "It felt different this time."

Also out of breath, he admitted, "It broke."

"What broke?"

"The condom."

I hit him in the chest. "Are you fuckin' serious?"

"Hey," he said. "I pulled out."

"Pulled out?" I jumped up. "People still get pregnant 'pulling out'. Don't ever do that shit again. I have enough shit on my roster. I don't need a baby."

Afraid, I went to Planned Parenthood and bought Plan B. Just in case that one little sperm found its way.

■　■　■　■

It was finals week and my period had been weird. For the first time in my life, I was spotting. That had never happened before. It was brownish and thick. After six weeks of that, I started cramping. I didn't have insurance, but I was in pain. I decided that after my last class exam, I was going to go to the emergency room and somehow figure out how to foot the bill.

I walked four blocks through the city streets, thinking they were going to tell me my ailment was stress related, and send me home with instructions to relax. Drink water. Some shit like that.

Entering the automatic double doors, I signed in at the security desk. I sat in the lobby with the druggies that fell and hit their elbows on the sidewalk and the ones who got into a fistfight and had gashes on their foreheads. I waited until my name was called. A brown-skinned girl with long braids and red nails weighed me, took my vitals, and asked me what I was in for. I told her I was spotting. She clicked the keys on the computer and then placed an identification bracelet on my wrist. Afterward I was taken to a small room. It was cold.

The doctor came in and asked some questions.

"I'm spotting and cramping," I told him.

"Any chance of pregnancy?"

I responded quickly and with surety. "No."

"Put this on." He handed me a gown. "Someone will come take you for tests."

The tests seemed never ending. First, they took blood. Then sent me back to the room. Next, they took me for an ultrasound. Then sent me back to the room. I sat there for a while wondering what was going on. Finally, a nurse came in and told me to lay back. She said she needed to insert a catheter. I was young. I didn't ask why. I laid back and opened my legs. She told me to relax. It was so cold. She tried to make small talk with me to get my mind off what she was doing, but it didn't work. I thought it was the most uncomfortable thing that I'd go through, having a tube stuck in me. After the catheter was in, a medical assistant took me to get another ultrasound.

Maybe I was dying. Still, I was too scared to ask.

I lay down on a hard steel exam table, catheter still dangling between my legs. The technician repeated the steps and squirted that gooey liquid on my abdomen. She pressed the apparatus into my stomach and massaged it around. I'm usually ticklish and would giggle, but this was no laughing matter. I felt like a piece of raw meat.

The tech pressed the apparatus further into my belly fat and stayed in one spot. She studied the monitor; I was still like a plank of wood.

The tech said nothing to me, as another girl came and rolled me into the discharge room.

Something was wrong.

The doc came in with some papers. He didn't even sit down.

"You're pregnant," he said without emotion.

"Excuse me?" I smiled an ugly smile. "Not possible."

"You're seven weeks pregnant." He laid the discharge papers near my leg.

"This is a mistake," I pleaded. "I'm in school."

It was like he wasn't even listening to me. "You're at high-risk for miscarriage since you're spotting and cramping."

I clutched my forehead. "I can't have a baby . . ." The last word trailed off.

"Here's some information about your options." He motioned to the papers. "You're discharged." And just like that, I was nineteen and pregnant.

A fuckin' statistic. My life. Over. God was punishing me for opening my legs. Because I wasn't a good Muslim girl, he got me. He got me good.

Even when the nurse popped the catheter out, I didn't flinch.

I got dressed and stood outside the double doors of the emergency room.

I called him. Wanting something. Comfort, perhaps. Reassurance.

"I'm at the hospital," I said quietly. "They say I'm pregnant."

For a long time, he didn't say anything. Then broke the silence. "Oh."

Hot tears rolled down my cheeks. "All you have to say is 'oh'? Fuck you."

There's a large chunk of time that I can't remember from this ordeal. I've learned that trauma can make you forget a lot of things.

■ ■ ■ ■

I went into autopilot and called around to different clinics. One quoted me $300 for an early-term abortion. They told me that I had to think it over for forty-eight hours before making an actual appointment. You know, just in case I changed my mind. I wasn't going to, but it was protocol.

I went back to my dorm and read all the pamphlets they gave me.

On my mattress, I lay on my side, gazing out the window at the people walking on campus with their seemingly perfect little college lives. I rubbed my stomach. Tears. "I'm so, so sorry." I told it. "But I can't. I can't be a mom. I don't know how to be."

I can't. I can't. I can't. I can't. I can't. I can't. I can't. I can't. I can't. I can't. I can't.

I repeated that over and over and over until I drifted off.

The appointment was set. He gave me $100, and I had some money left over from my tuition refund check. He came with me. We didn't talk the whole drive. He said nothing, didn't even try to talk me out of it. I signed in. He looked ill. I felt ill.

When they called me back, he didn't hug me, reassure me. He left, and I didn't know where he went.

The ladies at the clinic were nice. They tried to make me feel as comfortable as they could, given the situation. They made me sign papers. Lots of them. I signed without hesitation.

"You will vomit," one warned, handing me a vial of white pills. "And you will cramp. Take these exactly as directed. Any questions."

I shook my head. "No."

Just my luck, Mom was having a procedure done the very next day, and I was her designated driver. I picked her up, like a functioning zombie. I wanted to tell her, confess. But she'd be ashamed. Ashamed that I didn't learn from her mistakes. I'd hold onto my own burden. No need to put that heaviness on her.

The nurses took her in. I assured her the procedure would go smoothly and that I'd see her in a few. I started cramping again. Bad. I could barely sit in my seat. Sweat poured down my neck.

My great aunt arrived. "Are you okay?" She held a look of concern.

"I'm fine." I waved.

She smiled.

"I'm just gonna' go to the bathroom. Be right back," I said.

Only by the grace of God was I able to stumble to the bathroom. I guessed he liked me still, a little.

I sat on the toilet and hung onto the sink with one hand and with the other, the silver handicap bar. It was a single stall, so no one could hear my cries and prayers muffled by those four white walls. I imagined my uterus falling out. Tears for the pain. Tears for the shame. Tears for Mom and an aunt who had no idea what was occurring in the same building as them. Tears for being a bad Muslim. One who deserved every ounce of pain for booting the fetus and not giving it a chance.

Mom had had two abortions. One at fifteen. She had Big Sis not too long after. Then she got pregnant again. Another abortion. A few years later, she was pregnant with me. She didn't want me because she hadn't wanted any more children. And maybe she didn't want to be tied to my father. It's okay. I wouldn't want to be tied to someone like him either. She told me that I was to be given up for adoption right after birth. My grandma named me because Mom didn't want to. For some reason, the doctors fell in love with me. They said I was a pretty yellow baby. God intervened and touched Mom's heart. And I was kept.

I'm not sure how true this is, but according to the mother of one of my half-sisters, when I was a few months old, Mom tried to give me away again. She gave me to my fuck of a father, and he took me to his ex-wife's house.

"The momma don't want her," he said. "I'm taking her to the hospital."

"Don't punish the baby," she said. "It's not her fault she's here. You two made that decision. Take her back to her mother."

I guess Daddy did, because I was never in foster care.

When I looked down between my legs all I saw was deep crimson. Blood had seeped through my underwear and pants. My eyes rolled back as I began to shiver in disgust. I was going to bleed out and die, and I thought that maybe that wasn't such a bad thing.

I couldn't just sit there all day. Without looking in the toilet bowl, I flushed whatever came out of me. I cleaned the best way I could and pulled myself up using the sink. Every movement depleted my energy. I washed my hands of the blood.

I glanced up at the mirror and saw myself. The dark circles forming under my eyes, the dry, cracked lips, the curve in my spine; I hurt so bad that I couldn't even stand straight. I just needed to make it to the car. Drive to Target and get some fresh underwear and pants.

Everything was in slow motion. I was hyperaware of the hustling staff and patients moving back and forth. I stood in front of my aunt. She stared.

"I just started my period and bled right through my clothes." I gave a nervous chuckle. "I've got to go get some pants. Could you wait here for Mom? I'll be right back."

She nodded.

My legs were giving out. But I needed to get to the car. I don't remember how I got there. But I remember driving and barely keeping control. I was having what felt like contractions. I found a Target and almost fell out the car door. I wobbled to the entrance. All eyes must have been on me—the sickly woman, clutching her stomach. *Pants and underwear. Pants and underwear. Pants and underwear.* I made it past the theft detectors, and I knew that I couldn't walk anymore. I sat down on one of those motorized carts. I used it to drive around Target, and although I was still in pain, it offered much relief.

The next day, I was still very sick. Every time I took a pill, the contractions and more blood would come. I couldn't take it anymore, being alone. Being so embarrassed that I couldn't tell anyone. I finally broke down and confessed to my friend. She invited me over. We didn't talk about it. Just being in the company of someone gave me comfort. I was a little less alone.

The contractions came on so strong as I held my stomach and rushed to the bathroom. It didn't have a door, so I pulled the cloth curtain closed. I didn't push. Something came out and hit the water with a *thunk.*

Over.

I didn't want to see it. I didn't want that image in my head. I reached back and flushed.

I flushed it down the toilet.

I flushed my baby down the toilet.

The next week, I went to my follow-up appointment, alone. They put me on a bed and made me spread my legs. The doctor turned on a vacuum-like apparatus. It was loud and frightening. Just when I thought I was done with being a piece of raw meat, he suctioned me out.

"All done," he said, turning off the machine and patting my knee.

The nurse took me to this room with comfortable chairs lined up on each side. Several African American women were sitting in these chairs with blankets on their legs and heating pads on their stomachs, chatting casually like they had just got their nails done.

"Sit here," the nurse said. "Would you like some tea? It'll help settle your stomach."

I nodded. "Yes, please."

I got under the blanket and placed the heating pad on my stomach like the others. A huge wall-mounted TV played some ratchet daytime talk show. The nurse brought the tea with a smile and placed it in my hands. "Let me know if you need anything."

"The staff is so nice here," one girl with a long ponytail said to another girl with thick false lashes.

"Yeah, every time I come up in here, I get good service." Lashes blinked rapidly and took a sip from her Styrofoam cup.

Ponytail took the words right out of my head. "How many times?"

"Oh girl, this is like my third one," she said matter-of-factly. "I had two. Then I had my daughter. This is the third."

Another girl joined the conversation. "This is my second."

I sank further into my seat. And took a gulp of tea.

I was never, ever coming back. Ever.

5. MOM AIN'T MOM NO MORE

I left home at nineteen. Mom was becoming more and more possessive and tried to control me with money and other things to gain the upper hand. She used guilt and played the victim role, as she'd done with her family and children and the temporary men in her life. I was grown-ish and somewhat smarter. Her tactics no longer worked on me. I just wanted to be free of the suffocating world she'd created.

The day finally came. She had cut off my cellphone service while I was at a friend's house. After about twenty minutes on the line with Sprint, I figured it all out.

"Who the fuck does that?" I asked my girlfriend.

She just shook her head and shrugged.

The fire within me bubbled as I pushed the burgundy Ford Focus to 80 mph on the highway with no fucks given about the cops. Destination: home. I was about half an hour away, and it was go time. I was going to finally stick it to her. No more tucking my tail between my legs and cowering away. I'd grown a pair of hefty balls and I was going to use 'em. It had been years on top of years of bullshit, and I hadn't said a gotdamned word. She'd receive an occasional clap-back from me, but that was as far as I'd gone on the parental disrespect meter.

In my head, I went over the list of things I planned on saying to her:

1. *You always have fuck guys in and out the house trying to pretend to be my father.*
2. *You're bipolar as fuck. You flip out over little shit and start throwing shit around.*
3. *You're always telling me that I never do enough. I'm a fuckin' teenager trying to work and go to college and have a social life at the same damn time. So. Just. Fuck. Off!*

Since I was ten, she'd always tell me that if I didn't like the way things were run in *her* household that I had the option to leave. And I always wanted to reply: *how am I, as a ten-year-old kid, supposed to leave, with no job and no daddy? You sound really uneducated.*

But like a good, obedient child of God, I held it all in. I was grown now and had no other plan in place but hurting her feelings as she'd done mine all those years.

I barged in the side door, but then calmed down a bit because I was actually scared of the woman. I stepped lightly down the hall, my stomach in knots, and politely knocked on her bedroom door.

"Come in," she said.

I entered the dungeon—I mean, her room.

She sat on the edge of her bed, appearing calm, even while challenged by her teenage daughter. Mom was taller than me. The kind of woman that could rock a dress yet get underneath a car and fix an engine. She was sneaky and would attack physically if threatened. I knew that she knew exactly what the deal was, but I wasn't trying to get into a fight that night, so I kept it cool despite my prior plan to rip her ass.

"Mom, my phone is off." I tested the waters.

"Oh," she said nonchalantly, flipping her thick hair over her shoulder. "I turned that off."

My brow twitched, as I swallowed back the comet rising in my throat. "Why did you do that?"

She ignored my question and stood, towering over me. "I'm going to need the keys back to my car too."

"First of all, you turned my phone off while I was out. Anything could've happened! You couldn't have given me a heads-up?" My voice started to rise.

Her long arms crossed over her chest. "They're all *my* things."

"But it's my car too!"

"Well, it's in my name."

"It's in both our names!"

What really hurt my feelings was that I wasn't the worst teen in the world, and she treated me like one of her male trash-can niggas that she brought home. Like I was some kind of problematic child throwing my pussy at randos and snorting coke off butt cracks. I had a job. I paid for my car. I was in college.

"Fine," I said with tears flowing down my cheeks. "Take it all. I don't want nothin' from you."

I took her car key off my chain and placed it on the table, then left her room. She followed me down the hall, talking crap.

I remember being halfway up the stairs and looking down on her in complete fury when I couldn't handle her talking shit any longer. Even in anger, I noticed her perfect caramel complexion that matched mine and that condescending smirk on her face, like she'd just illustrated the cleverest bank heist the world had ever seen.

I never cursed at her or in front of her, like ever, in my life. And I had yuck mouth. But at that moment, I was full to the brim with everything nasty in the world.

"I'm. Sick. Of. This. Shit!" I screamed at her.

Her face didn't change. She was like a slab of marble. Or maybe that was a defense mechanism for her because her feelings had been compromised.

I stormed up the stairs, packed some of my shit, and disappeared into the night.

■　■　■　■

Little Sister doesn't know how to communicate well. Not with me. She reminds me of Mom so much that it's upsetting. They both fly off the handle so quickly and are too emotional. They can dish out but can never take a rebuttal. I'm very direct. No nonsense. My directness is too much for them. But I am who I am.

Somehow, Little Sister always catches me at my lowest moments and pushes me over the edge even more. You could say it's her gift. Dumping a pound of salt into a wound.

When she texts or calls, it's always something. I have to mentally prepare to deal with the information she's going to give me. Her delivery of bad information irks me. She'll sit on pertinent information for weeks, then dramatize the whole situation instead of just being direct, initially. When I deal with her by being frank, she thinks I'm insensitive, just like Mom. I don't care. Takes two to tango.

I'd just abruptly left my friend's house an hour earlier, alarming her. I had had an anxiety attack on her couch but couldn't articulate it. I'd gone home and plopped into bed, tired inside my head but restless.

Little Sister's text came in: *I need to see you guys face-to-face. Not trying to freak you guys out but don't ask questions.*

Already dead inside, irritation started to rise. I replied: *How can you not freak someone out if you're being secretive and dramatic?*

Deep down, I knew the drama and mystery were about my estranged mother, who I hadn't spoken to in about two years after I'd cursed at her and moved out. I just didn't want to deal with it.

■ ■ ■ ■

Let's rewind for a moment. Prior to my whole not-speaking-to-Mom-for-two-years debacle occurred, she had moved to Atlanta with my three younger siblings. I visited them twice. They seemed okay, but they weren't. Little Sister started to wild out. She was being foul and promiscuous, just like Mom was when she was younger. My brothers were trying to deal, but they had issues of their own. I couldn't be there. I didn't know how to be there, so I withdrew. I kept quiet.

Their house burned down. That put a tremendous amount of stress on the family. Older Sister and I were in Michigan. We called and tried to help, but Mom refused. Said she got it, when she really hadn't.

Mom began to break down physically. She was diagnosed with a genetic condition that fucks with her joints and bones. Little Sister has it too. Mom had surgeries on her toes first. She started taking pain meds. Her mind started to go. She began talking crazy and being irrational and erratic in her decision making. She cut off her own sisters, her mother, and aunt.

"I think Mom abuses pain pills," Little Sister told me once. "She's not right in the head."

We thought that if we gave her time, she'd heal. That God would heal her, release her from her own mind. If we just left her alone and let her blow off some pent-up steam, then everything would be good, like before, when she was a manageable kind of crazy.

Days turned into weeks. Weeks turned into months. And months into years with little to no contact. Eventually, they moved back to Michigan due to Mom's declining health. But the drama crossed state lines, along with their boxes and furniture. It must've called shotgun in the U-Haul.

Little Sister called me at two o'clock one morning, which was rare. I thought she was in danger because she lived a reckless life. I answered with fear in my voice.

She'd been crying. Could barely get a phrase out.

"What's going on?" I finally yelled.

"It's—it's . . ." More coughing. "Mom."

I sat up in bed, abruptly. "What?"

After she calmed down a bit, she recounted her story. "Her hair is thinning, so I spent money I didn't have to buy her some natural hair-care products. She's always asking me to do her hair, so I thought I'd surprise her for Mother's Day. She's been mad at me for the last week and not returning my phone calls, so I thought if I took the box over there, I could just leave it in front of her door.

"I drove over there and knocked and placed the box in front. She was there, but she wouldn't answer. I texted her and let her know that the box was there."

She stopped and sighed before continuing. "When I got home, she had texted me saying that she brought her gift back to my place and sat it outside in the front of the apartment building. I ran downstairs to find the box and it was gone. Someone stole it."

Little Sister burst out in tears again.

"Oh, no," I said. "I'm so sorry."

"She's been so mean lately. I had to go off on her because she started talking about my dad's death. I told her to never mention his name again."

Little Sister's father had just passed away. He died in a pool of his own blood. He had Alzheimer's and was always confused. His wife had left to run some errands, and he'd pulled out an IV and bled to death alone. I hadn't cared much for her father, but I could understand her grief. Plus, no one deserved to go out like that. A newfound anger twisted and vined around my heart for Mom. I knew she was declining, but to be mean to someone who was hurting was unacceptable.

"We're going over there tomorrow," I said.

"She's not gonna answer."

"I don't care. We're going."

I picked Little Sister up, and together we drove to Mom's apartment. We parked. Her car was there. It started to rain. The fat drops came down hard and fast.

I wanted to know why she hadn't gotten help. Why was she so mean? I was going to give her a piece of my mind, but then quickly decided against that. I wanted her to get well, so that we could salvage the relationship we had left. We needed her. Even as adults. We needed her.

"She's not gonna answer," Little Sister said, gazing at the wipers going back and forth. "I'm telling you."

"I have to try." I opened the door and zoomed to the tiny porch. My cell was in my pocket and getting wet. I stuck it in my bra, then pinned myself against the glass window. I buzzed her apartment. I banged on the door. I buzzed and banged. Hoping I'd hear her voice. Hoping that God had let some light into her dark mind. Hoping that she wasn't going to abandon me like Daddy had so many years ago.

I buzzed and banged.

I looked back at my sister. She shook her head from side to side.

She wasn't going to let me in. She'd cut me out as if I wasn't shit.

I emailed her the next day. Told her that if she didn't get help, then it was over. She was bullying my siblings. She was lying. Hurting people that didn't deserve it.

I told her that I'd been through therapy, and it worked. I told her that I'd help her go, take her, sit in the lobby, and wait for her.

She told me to mind my business about her mental health.

She'd made her choice.

Her mind was much stronger than any of us.

I opened my hand and let her drift away.

6. PLAYING HOUSE

I had done my duty as a Black child coming from a single-parent household. I'd fought against the odds. I got the stupid undergrad degree in business with the naïve idea that I'd be somebody with a good job right out of college. That my color hadn't mattered or that I was fat or Muslim.

I was dead-ass broke and called my grandfather, whom I'd never called for funds, and asked for $230 for a cap and gown, photos, and graduation fee. To my surprise, he sent the money without hassle. Maybe because I was the second one in the family to get a bachelor's and the first to get it in only three years and some change. I took upward of sixteen credits every summer. I wasn't playing. Nor had I wanted to be in college forever, like other people I knew. I hated college and yearned to get my life started.

My GPA was so-so, but I'd made it. I had plans. Big ones. Getting married, having kids, and settling down were never in those plans. Because of Mom, marriage repulsed me. I hated kids too. Kids may have hated me; I wasn't sure, because I hated them so much that I hadn't ever gotten the chance to ask them or ever cared about their response.

Our graduation was outside in a big football stadium. There was a sea of black and green and yellow. A huge screen facing us. We had a keynote speaker too. I remembered robotically clapping on cue to the inspirational things he said. I was a damn zombie with a pink scarf on and white Payless heels. Going through my mind was when the procession would end, so I could go home and sleep.

Since my last name is Vernon, I was near the end. I yawned as people's names were called. Then, finally, it was the business school's turn. I walked across the stage, was handed my temporary diploma, paused, and gave a picture-perfect smile, then walked offstage. I made a U-turn around the hundreds of seats and headed for the nearest exit.

Because I was antisocial throughout college, I had no one to congratulate or rejoice with. I hadn't made any friends or lifelong buddies. I was solo, bent on finishing and just leaving so I could check it off my list of things I should probably do in life. I passed a group of girls taking photos and jumping and screaming. And dads patting their sons on the backs. Cute, I thought, to have a daddy. Of course, mine wasn't present.

I was able to find my mom and siblings waiting for me with a single flower and a little graduation teddy bear holding a diploma. I thought that was cute. Mom and I had just gotten back on speaking terms. I gave them all hugs.

We returned to Mom's house, and my aunt came over. We ate Middle Eastern food and cake. I can't remember anything else from that day, except that I went home and passed out and didn't wake up until nighttime.

I had gotten a barrage of texts from non-school friends congratulating me. That also made my angsty heart smile. One happened to be from him. We hadn't spoken much since the procedure. It was a nice gesture; I rolled my eyes as I sent a text back saying thank-you. That text led to a meeting. More dates. And eventually, the same feelings returned. I was falling in love with him and his quiet nature and gentle gestures. His corny jokes and constant hunger for food and sex.

Love is something, to this day, I cannot really contain. Something I cannot explain. All I know is that it changed me. My goals. What I wanted in life.

We'd spoken about marriage briefly because it's such a huge thing in Islam. I honestly don't think you can be a true Muslim and not talk about it in some way or another. For many Muslims, it's the ultimate goal in life. To marry. Complete half of your deen. Your duty to God.

Even with all of that, I'd always say no when it came up. I'd seen all of Mom's marriages fail. All of Mom's friends' marriages fail. Then the ones who were married were being oppressed by possessive and toxic men—Muslim men who had superiority complexes and used religion to oppress their wives and daughters and sometimes sons.

Everyone in the Muslim community knew that we were together, although we never broadcasted it. It was taboo to showcase an unmarried union. His sisters started to hint about our relationship in front of their parents. His father obviously knew at some point. I feel like his mother was still a bit clueless, because to her, he was a golden child and could do no wrong.

I left my shared dorm room and moved into my very own crusty apartment with roaches, which was ten minutes from my old university. It was a month-to-month lease until I figured out what I wanted to do with my life or at least until I got a real job.

He'd come over and chill. Spend the nights on the weekend. We'd go to the movies and eat dinner. During the week, he'd go back home. Hear his family bitch about disappearing on the weekends. My friends and everyone else encouraged us to just get married.

I mean, I wanted to spend more time with him and I did love him. And he had asked before. But I was afraid. Afraid of losing myself. Afraid of getting married so early when the odds were against us.

We were driving around in his loud and raggedy car that he got for $700 from some dude in Detroit, and all of a sudden, I said, "I think you should tell your parents that we want to get married."

We were at a stoplight. One that seemed to last forever.

"What?"

"You heard me." I crossed my arms over my chest. "You've been asking me all this time, and now I'm agreeing. Let's tell your parents. Right now. Call them and see if they are home."

"This soon?" His eyes were big.

The light changed green. He pumped the gas.

"If we don't do this now, then it'll never happen."

He shook his head. Which, for some reason, enraged me.

"Pull over," I demanded.

"What? Why?"

"Pull over. I'm getting out and walking home."

"No, you're not."

I reached for the door handle. He swerved a bit, trying to keep me from opening the door while also navigating a vehicle.

"Fuck! Okay. I'll call them now." He said, "Happy?"

I grinned and nodded vehemently. It may have seemed like a forced proposal, but deep down, I knew he wanted to as well, but was just too scared to face his parents.

His dad answered the phone. "*Assalamualaikum*," he said in a low voice. "Abu, I'll be home in ten. Amerra is with me. We have something to tell you."

I didn't hear what his father's response was. Neither he nor I spoke to each other during that short ride. We were both scared shitless.

We walked up the crooked porch steps to his parents' house and removed our shoes upon entering the doorway. We saw his father first. I always loved his father. He was a gentle and kind man with a huge black beard and a big belly. He was always cooking and feeding anyone who came into his home. He had a strong Jersey accent, and one could hear his hearty laugh from far away.

He and I sat across from him and his mother.

"So, what's this about?" She asked no one in particular.

"Mom, we want to get married," he answered.

"Married?" She repeated.

His father chimed in. Perhaps my facial expression changed for the worst. "I think that's a good idea, but marriage is nothing to play around with. It's hard work. Y'all know that, right?"

We both eagerly shook our heads like we knew exactly what he was talking about.

His mom laughed. "He don't have nothing. You know that."

"I know that already." I made it my goal not to say it through gritting teeth.

"You just finished college and he just entered."

"I understand," I replied.

"In order to get married, a man has to have something to bring to the table."

She gave us her blessing, reluctantly. We all hugged. And we told them that the date was set for the following week.

We were getting married.

■　■　■　■

I decided to go to Hamtramck to visit a popular Bengali clothing store that sold prayer rugs, incense, hijabs, and traditional saris. The store was compact but was a Muslim's one-stop shop. Along the high walls, all the way to the top of the ceiling, were saris with beads and some with sequins. Deep reds and crimsons with gold and royal blues with sheer scarves to match. Muslim women during their weddings are by far the most beautiful, the most adorned. Marriage is such a sacred and celebrated occasion.

I'd already known that saris were expensive, and as a new graduate without a job and a whole-ass apartment to pay for, I wouldn't be able to afford anything fancy.

On the rack below all the pretty things were more affordable abayas. I went through, grabbing patterns that caught my eye. There was an olive green one with gold embroidery on the cuffs and a long black one with blue and silver crystals around the chest area. I took both inside the constricted fitting room with a cloth curtain that was supposed to shield my big Muslim body from the Yemeni store owner with a full orange beard dyed with henna who was behind the counter.

A cloudy mirror stood before me; I removed my shirt and studied the curves and dips and the stretch marks riding up my waist like brown lightning bolts. I prayed that one of the abayas fit. I wasn't that concerned about the color or style. Broke fat people didn't have the luxury of being cute and being able to get their arms through the sleeves. It was one or the other.

Luckily, I wasn't as fat as I thought I was, and both fit. I liked the black one with the blue accents better.

"How much is this one?" I held the abaya up.

"Eh," he said in a foreign accent, "that one is turty-fih."

I laid it on the counter and pulled crumpled cash from my purse. I wasn't grown enough to buy a legitimate wallet or place my bills the right way, but I was old enough to get married.

He placed my wedding dress in a bag. Then gave me the Islamic greeting, *Assalamualaikum*, as I walked out the door.

No one was involved with my wedding. There weren't any friends fawning over me about which colors I should choose for the reception. There were no ugly puke-green bridesmaid dresses with floofy shoulders. I wasn't able to be a Bridezilla like the ones on that TV show and bitch about how everything was just falling apart at the last minute, while my mom fanned me on a pretty white couch as tears of frustration fell from my delicate prebridal eyes.

I was on autopilot like I always am. Get dress. Get married. That's all.

It never occurred to me that including everyone in this occasion and proper planning should've been mandatory.

Mom never had an actual wedding before. She would just bring men home and be married, or she'd have something very tiny and informal with just us kids, three witnesses (mandatory for an Islamic wedding), and an imam (spiritual leader of a mosque).

The night before our wedding, he and I decided to talk a nice stroll past the burned-down houses, barking dogs, and smashed sidewalks along our street. I mean, it was our neighborhood now, until we found something better, so we needed to get better acquainted with our surroundings. The plus of living in that dump was that it was close to his college and close to my new job as a manager at Walgreens.

Life was good.

Because we've had countless heated all-night arguments throughout the duration of our relationship, I can't even remember what started this particular one. But the usual topic of arguments consisted of money or religion or his whereabouts.

At the end of the block, I yanked my hand from his.

"I don't want to marry you," I screamed as I stormed back toward the apartment.

He stood there. Angry. "Good, cuz actually, I don't want to marry you either."

I spun around. Thinking that just maybe he was going to fight for me.

Nodding with tears in my eyes, I said, "Oh, so it's that easy, huh?"

Silence.

"The wedding is off." After I said that, I started running. I got inside the apartment and locked the door behind me.

Once he realized he'd left his car keys in the house, he started banging on the door, asking me to let him in. I wasn't letting him in for shit. My feelings were hurt. So, I sat with my knees in my chest as he knocked and called my phone repeatedly. Until it just stopped.

The next day, I woke up with a headache from crying all night. I definitely wasn't going to be with someone who hadn't wanted to be with me and wouldn't fight to keep me. He was weak, and I hated him.

Now, I was going to have to call my sister and tell her not to come. That the wedding was off. That I had failed at my first marriage before it even began. That I was just like Mom. I couldn't keep a man. It must've been in our DNA. Anti-men marriage failers.

He called me.

I hadn't answered.

He called again. No answer.

He texted: *Stop playin and answer the phone.*

I didn't respond. I was so exhausted that I fell back asleep.

I awoke to banging on my window. I lived in the hood and leaped out of bed, thinking someone was trying to break in. Seconds later, there was more banging at the front door.

"Who is it?" I yelled in an aggressive voice.

"It's the boogey man." It was him.

I opened the door. Ready to cuss him out. Punch him. Whatever.

Before I could say anything, he grabbed me, wrapping his arms around my entire body tight. Planting me with kisses on my cheeks and head and mouth.

"I'm—mad—at—you," I got out, in between the kisses.

"So what?" he said. "We have a wedding tonight."

"You said you didn't want to marry me anymore."

"You said it first. I was mad. And that was last night." He smiled. "You got something to eat? I walked a long way to get here."

■　■　■　■

I wore my black abaya with the blue and silver accents on the chest and cuffs. It was way too big for me, but I felt pretty. His mom came, his dad, his older sister that I hated, and my older sister came in the nick of time. My mom wasn't coming. In her voice over the phone, I knew she was displeased by my choice. He hadn't had anything to give me. But I was marrying him whether she liked it or not. Plus, who was she to judge. She couldn't even keep a man herself. I planned on being different.

We all sat on the dark red carpet in my very empty living room because I hadn't had the money for real furniture or even fold-up chairs.

All I had was him, and that was enough. I'm sure he felt the same way.

He wore a white thobe that was also too big for him. He'd liked borrowing clothes from one of his friends that was clearly way larger than him.

We sat cross-legged together as his father started the ceremony with all of our witnesses. His father asked what my dowry was. I hadn't thought about it. Dowries are huge in Islam, and if one isn't given, then the marriage isn't even valid. Some popular dowries are land, cows, gold, money. Extravagant shit like that. But I knew that he had none of that.

So, I asked for a ring in the amount of $500 when he got on his feet.

Then that was it. We were married. We were legit.

We hugged everyone; then they left.

No cake cutting. Or gift table. No white dress or bouquet toss. But I hadn't cared because I could now have lawful sex with the person I loved.

And we had lawful sex many times that evening. We could claim each other in public now, without side eyes from other Muslims. We could play house. I'd support him in whatever way I could until he graduated, and then he'd be able to take care of me fully. We had plans. Big plans.

My identity as the girl who wanted to travel solo and detested anything that included family or marriage or pregnancy talk crumbled completely as "I" turned into "we," as "we" turned into "he."

■　■　■　■

I had no idea what being a wife was, what it looked like. What it was supposed to feel like. I was fuckin' nineteen! I just thought if you loved someone enough, were a good Muslim, then God favored you and was like, "Imma make this easy for them because these people know how to follow the rules."

We constantly argued about money and time. He wasn't bringing in enough of it. Well, none at all. And his time, to me, was spent lollygagging, while I was holding down all the bills and food and gas, while he was down the street playing basketball with his friends and participating in amateur MMA fights on the weekends.

Was this what marriage was? I had already struggled alone. Struggling with an added person sounded like hell. Sounded much like parenting. I morphed into a parent. An angry one. I felt old, way past my years.

We loved hard, but we also hated each other hard. It was this back-and-forth pull of control. He wanted the submissiveness that Muslim women supposedly owed to Muslim men. And I wanted an actual man, maybe one who goes in on half the rent sometimes.

The thing about the Muslim men that I knew was that they always wanted obedience without bringing anything to the table. They expected the woman to be the whole package, while they lounged around expecting to be fed grapes from a vine. Muslim women, Black women, have been carrying dudes on their backs for hundreds, maybe even thousands of years. Maybe it's in our DNA to take on everything and make life easy for others as we burden and bury ourselves.

So, I fell in line and I did it too. With complaints, of course, but I held my man down as a good Black, Muslim woman was expected to.

I even had to teach him how to write a check. I looked at him like he was crazy when he stared down at the check blankly, the pen hovering over the empty line. I thought he was kidding at first, because he was always playing. "Are you serious?" I scoffed.

He hunched his shoulders. "My parents never taught me."

"Here," I said, taking the pen from his chubby fingers. "This is where you write down the number of the amount in words."

He didn't know how to construct a résumé. By then I didn't have to ask. I'm sure his parents missed that one too. He brought me a flyer one day. The airport was hiring. Together we went to the library to create his résumé because neither of us had or could afford laptops. I asked him about his previous work experience. He goofed around and tried to tickle me as I typed away.

"Boy, if you don't stop playing." I swiped his hand away. "Do you want this job or not?"

"Okay, okay, okay." He sat up straight. "Ask me again."

After his résumé was finished, and I fluffed up some shit, he turned it in. He didn't really know what an interview entailed because it was his first real job, so we had a mock session. I was the interviewer. I told him what to say and what not to say. Firm handshakes. Keep eye contact. Sit up straight. All the good stuff.

He was called in for an interview. His car was broke, yet again, so I drove him half an hour away and dropped him off at the front door. He gave me a kiss on the cheek, and I wished him luck.

Two hours later, he called me to come pick him up. He was holding a folder.

"I'm now an employee of the airport!" He hopped in.

I was very excited for him. I was excited that he could now pay rent. Groceries. Get his own car instead of using mine.

None of that would end up happening because he was hired as a part-time employee.

He assured me that all of the money issues were temporary. He'd graduate with a degree in education in three years, and then he'd take over all the bills. That dream sounded nice.

PART 3
LIFE, UNFILTERED

7. CAGED IN

"Slut," he seethed.

As he added fuel to the fire, I tore apart the living room. Then I attacked him. He pinned me to the carpet.

"If you don't let me go, I'll kill you!" I screamed.

He laughed as if I'd just told him a funny story, which enraged me even more. I told him that I didn't like guns, but he kept bringing them into the house. He let me go and taunted me. I tore apart the closet and grabbed loose bullets. I started to throw them at his head.

Then I grabbed the actual gun.

Air rushed through flared nostrils. My chest heaved. Heart pounded against my ribs. Sweat beads dripped along my hairline. The collar of my shirt was ripped. I stood at the bathroom door with a shotgun in my hand, not knowing whether it was loaded or not.

By then, he had already called 911.

"I'm hiding in the bathtub!" he screamed into the phone at the operator. "She's out there with a gun. Hurry!"

I banged the butt of the gun against the door.

I just wanted to talk to him.

The police came. A Black cop and a white one. They stepped inside and commented on the knocked-over television set and tipped chairs. I stood there with a baby face and a natural pout.

"One of you has to leave," the officer said.

They escorted him to the room to grab some clothes. Before he and the officers left, he said, "It's over between me and you."

I held it together until the door was shut and their footsteps died. I stood there, staring at the door for a long time before I collapsed.

■   ■   ■

I lay on the cold sand on a manmade beach in Detroit in that same black abaya with blue and silver studs decorating the neck and chest. The one I got married in a few years before. The skirt part was hiked up past my knees, exposing dingy black pants. I'd worn that same outfit a million times since he'd left to stay at his mom's place a week prior. I gazed into the sky of clouds, wondering how far they could travel.

The cool, salty air from the water rushed over my body. Tears flowed along the side of my face and submerged themselves in the sand, creating little moisturized orbs. I was so fucked up; I'd been fucked up for a long time and hid it so well. But it kept rearing its ugly head. I'd lost control and grabbed an actual gun. What had I been thinking?

I couldn't blame any of my problems on depression or anxiety or schizophrenia because my people, my community wouldn't accept it. Where I came from, mental illness didn't exist in a good Muslim's life. Religious and law-abiding Muslims were never touched by those kinds of issues. Succumbing to mental illness was a sign of a weak Muslim, a sinner. Because you weren't a strong enough Muslim, steadfast in your faith, then God was punishing you. He was punishing me.

I had been dealing with mental breaks throughout my entire adolescence and young adulthood. One time in college, I was so overwhelmed, drowning in worries, that my legs collapsed underneath me, and I just lay on the shower floor, sobbing uncontrollably. I'd also have outbursts of anger if I felt attacked or ridiculed. One time some friends were making fun of me, just jokes, and I got so mad, so angry, that I hopped in my car and tried to run them over. They jumped out of the way, and my car ended up on the sidewalk. During panic attacks, my heart would beat so furiously against my chest that I'd feel like I was going to die, right then and there, of a heart attack.

But even with all of these instances, I would never allow myself to claim mental illness or seek real help. It was taboo, so I—and many others—suffered silently and hoped that nothing too bad happened. When I would confess that I was going through "stuff," I'd have people dismiss me, tell me that if I'd prayed more, done more religious acts, asked God to make me right and normal, then I wouldn't be experiencing pain, trauma. That it'd all just drift away.

I believed. So, I never got the help that I needed.

In my mind, I'd failed. I had a college degree, but I was stupid. I was photogenic, but I was ugly on the inside and on the outside. No one liked me. I was evil. The devil incarnate. I was incapable of loving or being loved. *That's why Daddy left you so easily, because no one loved you. Not for real. It was why your friends wouldn't help you because you're a bitch. You're too fat to fit into normal clothes. Why are you even on this planet? You are a waste of space. Why did God bring you here? If you died, no one would even notice. Maybe you should've just died.*

I sat up and dialed Mom.

"*Salaams?*"

I couldn't speak. The greeting stuck in my throat.

"Hello?" she said. "Amerra? Are you okay?"

It felt like a long time before I whispered, "No, Mom. I'm not, actually."

She talked. I cried silently, but I knew she heard the sniffles. I listened. I heard her, but it wouldn't penetrate. It couldn't. The negativity, the fucked-up stuff in my mind was so much stronger than anything she could've ever said.

"You need to talk to somebody."

"I'm gonna admit myself," I said, "to a hospital."

"Oh, Amerra." With hurt in her voice, she sighed.

There was a pause. Then she asked, "You don't want to hurt yourself, do you?"

I shook my head. "No, Mom." I hadn't known for sure though.

"I want you to know that I'm always here and that I love you."

"Love you too. Bye."

I got up, dusted my abaya off, and grabbed my flip-flops. My eyes ached, my head hurt, and I hadn't eaten in days. I planned on going home and resting before I packed my bag and took a trip to the hospital's psych ward.

None of my friends called me. Reached out. Even though they knew what had happened. So, I decided to contact one, hoping for some kind of support.

"Hey," I said over the receiver.

"Hey," she replied. "What's going on?"

I took a deep breath. "He left and I'm kinda messed up about it. I don't think I'm gonna' make it."

She replied, "Oh." I wasn't sure if she was just uninterested or maybe didn't know what to say, but it pissed me off.

"Well, I gotta go," I mumbled.

I called another friend and asked if I could visit. She brushed me off, too, saying that she didn't know if she was going out on a date or not.

So, I lay in bed. When I awoke, it was the next day. The sun shone through the blinds and into my face. I got up and figured that I needed to eat. I made a bowl of cereal. I loved cereal and usually could eat an entire box in one sitting. Fruity Pebbles sloshed around in the milk as I sat alone at the kitchen table. I put the spoon to my mouth and began to chew. The movement was foreign to me. I instantly got sick and spit everything out. I flushed the cereal down the toilet and tossed the bowl and spoon into an empty sink.

As I began packing the essentials, I thought about what my reputation would be after being admitted. The crazy Muslim girl who wasn't strong enough to withstand life. She wasn't close enough to God. "That's why this and that" type conversations would be had. Then I started thinking about other options and remembered Mom said that I needed to talk to someone. I Googled mental health for Muslims and *Muslim Family Services* popped up. I called. If they said no or gave me a ridiculous price to pay or couldn't see me that day, then I was going to admit myself. Rationality was quickly dissipating.

A girl with a Middle Eastern accent answered. She was pleasant and treated me like a human. That was nice. She transferred me to an on-call counselor.

"Muslim Family Services," the counselor greeted.

"Hi, my name is, ergh, Amerra," I stammered. "I'm having some issues and I wanted to know if I could come in today."

"What kind of issues?"

My smile faded. "Like, mental."

"Okay. Are you having suicidal thoughts?"

"No, but I believe I should probably go to the hospital."

"Come in today at 2 p.m. We'll talk and go from there. Sound good?"

With an overnight bag full of clothes and toiletries for my trip to the looney bin, I didn't have much hope that the counselor could "cure" me of my depression. I had some deep-rooted shit swirling around in my head that'd take years to chip at, and I was giving her one session.

The place was a two-family flat in the heart of Hamtramck. The Muslim organization turned it into an office space where they fed the community, provided counseling services, and gave charity and shelter if needed. I rang the doorbell, and a young girl with a hijab answered. "*Wasalam*," she said. "Do you have an appointment?"

"Yes, I'm here to see the counselor."

She stepped to the side and ushered me in. "Oh yes, come, come."

I took a seat in the tiny waiting room where a huge box of clothes waited to be delivered to the needy and a children's old playhouse sat idle.

The girl yelled, "Your two o'clock is here."

Seconds later, a tiny, brown-skinned Somali woman emerged from around the corner with a smile. "Amerra, right?"

I nodded.

"Come with me."

She shut the door and took a seat behind her computer desk. Her eyes were big, and her teeth were straight and prominent. A colorful scarf was wrapped snug around her face and hair. She cupped her hands and then asked, "What can I do for you?"

I shifted in my seat. All of a sudden, it wasn't comfortable anymore.

"I, uh, I've lost everything. . . . And I don't have anyone to turn to—"

Her already big eyes became larger with compassion. I put my head down and began to weep. She got up from behind her desk and grabbed a box of tissues, then with her small hand, rubbed my shoulder.

"It's okay. Get it out."

I hated crying in front of other people, so I sucked it up and stopped.

"What have you lost?" She sat back down.

"My husband left. I lost my job a few months ago. My family— they are nonexistent and my friends . . ." I sighed, dabbing my eyes with the tissue. "I don't think I should be here."

Her eyes narrowed. "Explain? I don't understand."

"When I was little, I always asked God why was I on this earth. That I only caused problems for people. I was a nuisance. I wished I was never born."

"A problem for who?"

I grinned because that's what I did when I hit on a topic that I'd rather not touch. "Mom. My dad."

"Okay," she said thoughtfully.

"I have the same thoughts now. I'm not shit. I'm never going to be shit. It's over. I can't be helped."

Her brows crinkled. "Are you Muslim?"

I nodded. Barely.

"Do you have a degree?"

"Yes."

"In what?"

"Business."

"Hobbies?"

"Yeah." I sniffed. "I write stories."

"Oh, so you're creative?"

"I guess."

"Give me your hand." She held out hers.

I wasn't comfortable with personal touch, but I flopped my big hands in her little ones.

"You are Muslim. You are educated. You speak well. You are talented. You are beautiful even through your puffy eyes. You can be helped. It is not over. It's not going to be easy. Life never is. But it's not impossible. Are you with me?"

My bottom lip jiggled as I tried to fight back the waterworks. "Yeah. I'm with you."

She pulled out a pen and scribbled down a number and slid it across the table. "This is my personal number. Call me anytime. And I want to see you twice a week, every week, until we can figure something out."

■   ■   ■   ■

He and I had been back together for about six months since the gun and police incident and my therapy stint. . I was halfway through my master's program and working full-time for the state. Things were going mostly well, steady, but as usual we fell back into our comfort zone of verbal abuse and passive aggression, which turned into real aggression.

That day, the rain came down really bad. I was coming home from visiting my aunt. My friends had asked me if I wanted to hang out, but I declined. I planned on taking him to the movies, doing something special, since he worked a lot and we never got to see one another.

I got out of the car, water splashing everywhere as I rushed to the front entrance of our apartment building. Every time my rescue kitten, Kitty Boo Boo, heard the door open, she'd rush to greet me by rubbing her body against my ankle. She was my baby, with her little black spots and white body like a little cow.

Upon entering, I gave hubby a kiss on the cheek. He was watching TV, under a knit blanket on the couch, where he could usually be found.

"I'm going to get changed," I told him, removing my wet scarf.

He shrugged.

It was hard to get his attention when the TV was on.

As I changed, my stomach started to cramp. My period was around the corner. Ugh.

I returned to the living room with a jacket stuffed under my arm. "Ready?"

He looked me up and down. The way he looked at me, you would've thought that he'd just viewed a sex tape with me and one of his best friends.

Grimacing, he said, "I'm not going anywhere with you dressed like that."

I sat the jacket on the table and surveyed my ensemble. A black lace shirt that hit midthigh, a long-sleeve turtleneck underneath that, black pants, and of course, hijab.

"What are you talking about? I wear this all the time." I argued.

"You look like a slut." He turned the volume up.

Slut rang through my ears. The man that I loved. Who I thought loved me. Just called me a slut. Again. *Slut*: Noun. Derogatory. A woman who has many sexual partners. A woman with low standards of cleanliness. *Synonyms:* promiscuous woman, prostitute, whore, tramp, hussy, harlot. He was the only man I'd ever slept with, and I was a slut because I wore pants?

Usually, when he called me names, I'd find some reason to not go crazy. My therapist was helping me manage the anger that stemmed from all the trauma that occurred prior to the marriage. But I'd taken two diet pills that day, which had already fucked with my temperament, and my hormones were raging from God's little monthly gift.

I snapped.

Although it pains me to admit, I attacked him. Again. I got on top of him and punched any place I could find. I was savage. On a rampage. All the things that ever happened to me in life erupted, and he was the main target. Somehow, he managed to pin me to the ground. Breathing hard, he told me that I was crazy. He grew tired and took his weight off my chest. As I lay on that beige carpet, I looked up at the ceiling.

Kitty Boo Boo didn't care for loud noises. The fighting had frightened her, so she ran off and hid under the couch. That's the only thing I actually felt bad about.

I finally sat up, crying and hyperventilating. "Get the fuck out. Just leave. This isn't going to end well. I'm not going to stop."

His response was a condescending grin. "I'm not going anywhere. This is my fuckin' house."

A newfound anger source was unleashed. I grabbed the bleach spray and grabbed the coat I'd bought him for Eid and sprayed it down. I opened the front door and started tossing his shoes out into the shared hallway while screaming, "Get out!" Over and over again. And when that didn't work, I started grabbing his clothes from the closet. He didn't like that. He wrestled the clothes out of my hands and pushed me to the ground. I grabbed his ankle, and he ended up falling too. He crawled away and grabbed a hanger. He threw it at my face, and it hit me in the eye. The pain was horrendous. I rolled around in the pile of clothes, eye watering, screaming bloody murder. He tried to console me, but I shoved him away.

"Why couldn't you just leave like I asked you?" I asked, holding the pinched teary and very red eye. "I'm calling the police."

I rushed into the bedroom and locked the door. He banged and banged. I fake-dialed the cops and pretended to tell them that he'd assaulted me. I heard him run out the door and start the engine. I peeked out the window; finally, he was leaving. That's all I wanted. To be alone.

Clothes were everywhere. Kitty Boo Boo was still in hiding. And I was drained. I had spazzed and was now coming down from the anger high. I picked up my cell and called a friend.

"Hello?"

"Girl." I sighed. "We just got into it again."

I envisioned her shaking her head. "You okay? Where's he at?"

"I'm good. He hit me in the face with a hanger, though." My eye was swollen. "I think he left."

At that moment, blue and red lights flashed through the bedroom window. I slid off the edge of the bed with the phone wedged between my shoulder and ear. "Oh God," I whispered.

"What?"

"The police are here."

I watched two white policemen get out of the car and go up to an electric blue car.

Hubby's car.

He'd never left.

"I gotta go." I didn't even wait for her to respond. I let the phone fall to the floor.

Rushing to the front door of our apartment, I cracked it and listened. Kitty Boo Boo came out and stood next to my ankle.

"She scratched my face," I heard him say.

I hadn't even scratched him. I punched him. That was like two entirely different things. And furthermore, he didn't tell them what he'd done to me. As I argued with myself, Kitty Boo Boo took her chance and slid through my legs and toward the policemen.

"Kitty Boo Boo," I yelled and chased after her, stepping over all his shoes that I had tossed into the hall.

She stopped right in front of them. Her green eyes widened. The policemen flashed the light in my face. I squinted, shielding my eyes with my forearm.

Delirium hit. What was I going to say? What was I going to do?

I grabbed the cat, leaped over the shoes, and scurried back into the unit like the Hunchback of Notre Dame.

Seconds later, there were three heavy knocks on the door. My heart raced, but the police had been called on me before. All I had to do was be smart, calm, and finesse my way out of the situation. I opened the door and smiled. One of my eyes was still swollen, but overall, I was cute.

Both officers surveyed the shoes near the doorstep.

"Ma'am," Officer #1 said. "What's going on?"

Meanwhile Officer #2 entered the home and measured the damage. Didn't he need a warrant or something?

I shook my head in bewilderment and scrunched my brows. "Nothing really. Just a simple disagreement."

"He says that you scratched his face, you poured bleach on his coat, and tossed his shoes out." He pointed to the shoes in the hall for dramatic effect.

"You know what. I bought him that coat, so technically it's still mine and the shoes—" I started picking them up one by one and tossing them back in. "—I can just grab them all pretty easily."

Officer #1 started looking through the coats on the rack and stopped at the one that I'd sprayed cleaner on. He motioned for Officer #2 to smell it. "Smells like bleach to me."

"That's destruction of property, whether or not you bought it. It's *his* coat."

"But—"

Officer #1 said, "You've lied and told us that nothing happened, and you've admitted to spraying bleach on his coat. He called us, and you're going to jail."

I stood back. "Okay. Okay. We got into a fight. I threw all his shit out there. I just wanted him to leave. Did he tell you that he hit me in the eye with a hanger? Huh? And look, I've got scratches on my arm."

"You had your chance to tell us your story when we first asked you." He pulled out the cuffs.

Somehow, I had my phone in my hand and I dialed Mom really fast.

"Hello?" Sleep was still in her voice.

"I'm going to jail," I said and dropped the phone.

Reality didn't hit until he cuffed me. That cold metal against my skin. The heaviness. The way it clanked as he adjusted the cuffs around my thin wrists.

My eyes were barely open because I was boo-hoo crying. I mean, I was crying hard. In passing, I saw him. My husband. He wore a look of defeat as he sat halfway in the driver's seat and halfway out. I said nothing to him.

"Watch your head," Officer #2 told me as he guided me into the back of the cruiser.

They got in and we pulled off.

Snot and tears covered my face. I know I looked crazy. "Wait!" I yelled.

Officer #1 looked back at me.

"Please pull back around. I have to tell him about the cat. She's my baby." The last word trailed off.

For some reason, the officer did as I requested.

He rolled the window down. I screamed, "Take care of Kitty Boo Boo. Please. Don't hurt her!"

■ ■ ■ ■

I was ushered in through the back door of the precinct. They uncuffed me and passed me on to another male officer, who was young and, of course, white, but still intimidating. He placed me in a small cell, kind of like the ones that circus people use to transport a lion or a monkey. I sat on the small bench, streams of tears on my face, whimpering. My hands were clasped, and my foot jiggled with anxiety as the officer prepared the camera for my very first mugshot.

He stood at the opening of the cell with a smooth face and blue eyes. "I'm going to fingerprint you and take your photo. You've gotta remove your jacket and scarf."

"But I'm Muslim." I sniffled.

With hesitation, he said, "I've gotta call the supervisor."

"Do you at least have a female officer?"

"There are no female deputies on shift tonight." He picked up the phone.

When the supervisor answered, he turned his back to me and spoke low. After a few seconds, he hung up the phone and returned to the puffy-eyed mess that was me.

"He says you've got to remove everything. Even your scarf. It's policy."

It was a bad time for me to play revolutionist. I was at their mercy. The mercy of a white man who didn't care about my religious beliefs. All he saw was a criminal.

I burst out crying as I slowly removed my jacket, exposing my arms and the upper part of my chest. My hijab was last. I slid it off and handed it to him. The tears came full force as I stood before him half-naked. He didn't offer me a tissue or tell me that things like this happened all the time. He just took my hand and pressed each finger on the scanner. One by one, until all ten were in the system.

The last phase was the photo. The mugshot.

"Face forward," he called out from behind the camera.

My body shivered. *Click. Flash.*

"Turn to the right." *Click. Flash.*

"The left." *Click. Flash.* "Step this way."

When I got nervous or scared, I always had to take a shit. "I've got to use the bathroom."

"Okay," he said and led me to a semi-hidden nook.

No door. Nothing. He backed up and stood in the opening, crossing his arms over his chest. The toilet was about three feet away from him. I hesitated for what seemed like years, my eyes bouncing back and forth from his uniformed back to the silver toilet. I knew he'd grow tired and rip me from the nook if I didn't make a decision soon. I pulled my pants down, mid-knee, and sat on the toilet while watching him intensely. Waiting for him to turn around and stare. I didn't trust cops. I sat there for a few seconds, but nothing came out. I couldn't get past him just standing there, listening to the tinkles of my pee hitting the water in the bowl. I just couldn't do it.

I pulled my pants back up. "Never mind," I said.

Afterward, he passed me a scratchy beige blanket, which I used as a makeshift covering for my hair and arms.

He led me to my final holding place. Before he slammed the door, I asked, "How long will I be in here?"

"It's Saturday, so you'll be here until the judge gets in on Monday, but we'll try and get you a cell with a cot in the morning."

I was locked in a concrete holding cell with another bathroom nook with no door and a camera facing it. The walls were scrawled with graffiti in red, green, blue, and black pen and marker. People's phone numbers, gang signs, lazily drawn dick figures, and signatures from yesteryear's prisoners. Shockingly, there was no odor, probably because it was so cold. Which would later prove to be an issue. The blanket was too little to cover my entire body. I sat down on the concrete bench and cocooned the upper part of my body. It still didn't protect me from the chill, but it was better than nothing.

Sitting in that cell, I wasn't so much angry as I was disappointed in myself and in my relationship. I kept going over how I came to that point. How someone who worked full-time, maintained her mental illness when no one really knew about it and was in a master's program, ended up in jail for domestic violence.

And Kitty Boo Boo. I'd left her. She was probably wondering where her mama went. I failed.

I'd been in therapy for a while. While I was in the pen, I thought about some coping mechanisms I'd learned. I'd choose a happy thought and fixate on that because it was going to be a long weekend. I couldn't focus on the man who put me in jail. I couldn't focus on possibly being fired from my job or being kicked out of my program. I chose one thought. One image.

Kitty Boo Boo.

Her little black-and-white body. Her pink nose and greenish eyes. How she always tried to sit on my face at night. How she took her afternoon naps in my tub of colorful hijabs hidden away in the back of the closet.

I lay down on the hard bench and said her name in my head over and over again until I drifted to sleep. I'd awake every so often to the echoes of my own snores and be jarred back to the sad reality of incarceration. My body was stiff from the hardness of the bench. I'd turn over every twenty minutes, so my bones wouldn't ache. I prayed for that cot and cell. Anything was better than what I had currently.

There was a phone near the door. I only knew my sister's and Mom's number by heart. I called them, but every attempt was unsuccessful. The phone would always cut off near the connecting part. I'd hang up and lie back down. Fall asleep. Wake back up and try again. In between, I hung onto positive thoughts. At one point, I wondered why I wasn't madder. I mean, I'd always been an angry person, but I was shockingly at peace.

After a few hours, I gave up and called him. The phone connected.

"Hello?" he said.

"I need you to call my mom. Tell her I'm in jail. Tell her to bring my medications," I was on a vitamin regimen and diet pills. I spoke quickly, because I didn't know how long I had to talk.

All he said was, "Okay." He sounded tired.

"Bye," I whispered.

They brought another prisoner in. He was screaming. I rushed to the door and watched them toss him in the cell across from me. He looked crazy as fuck. He was old, with white hair that stuck up in every direction like Einstein's. He kept yelling unintelligibly. He got up fast and rushed the door. I leaped back, even though I was safe behind a locked door.

I started cramping really bad. So I sat on the toilet, knowing that some officer was probably watching me. In the seat of my pants were streaks of blood. The worst time to start my period. I looked around, and there was no tissue either. I turned on the faucet. It sputtered rusty water. I wet my undies and used that as a towel.

I banged on the door. "Hello? Anyone out there? Hello!"

A different officer's face appeared in the circular window. Looked like I was bothering him and his important desk work.

"I'm on my period. I need a pad and tissue."

He left without saying anything. A few minutes later, he unlocked the door and brought me a sanitary napkin and the smallest amount of tissue humanly possible.

I mustered a smile. "Thanks."

Maybe an hour later, the phone rang. I answered, "Hello? Hello?"

"Amerra?" It was Mom's voice.

"Mom, I've been trying to call you all night."

"I know. The phone kept disconnecting," she said. "Are you okay?"

"I'm fine. I'll be here till Monday, they said."

"The charges have been dropped. I talked to them on the phone a few minutes ago. They're processing the paperwork now."

You'd think I'd be ecstatic. That I'd leap in the air like at the end of some '80s montage. I was stoic. I'd been through so much in the last eight hours that I didn't even have the energy to delve into any more emotions. I'd been carved out. Demeaned by my husband and stripped in front of the officers. Even though, I would be free, I really wasn't.

An officer unlocked the door and brought in a Styrofoam cup of Crystal Light and a packaged honey bun. He handed it to me.

"When do I get to leave?" I asked.

"Soon," he said and shut the door.

I placed the cup and honey bun beside me. I was hungry, but I didn't eat stuff like that.

Half an hour later, the door was unlocked again. "Let's go." An officer motioned for me to get up.

Just like that, I signed some papers and was free.

I called him. Asked if he could pick me up. I waited in the lobby. People entered, inquiring about loved ones who'd been arrested. For the ones who didn't have the funds to bail them out, they exited in a rush. Off-duty officers left, headed home after a long night of patrolling and arresting.

Unable to wait inside the precinct any longer due to claustrophobia, I stepped outside into the chilled morning air. Cars whizzed back and forth, getting their Saturday morning to-do lists complete. Kids had karate practice. White people enjoyed brisk walks, while others jogged.

He pulled up. I took the walk of shame to the car. I got in the passenger side. Pulled the squeaky door shut. For a long time, we just sat there. In silence. As he pulled onto the main street and headed for home, there was so much I wanted to say. I'm sure it was the same for him.

We were halfway there. "You okay?" he asked.

I didn't look at him and swallowed. "I just got out of jail."

"I didn't press charges."

"You lied," I said calmly.

"I didn't lie," he protested.

"You fuckin' lied," I said. "You didn't tell them what you did."

His voice rose. "I was scared. I didn't know what to do. Things happened so fast."

"But you lied." I started to cry.

"Look, it wouldn't have done anybody any good for both of us to be in jail."

I pinched my eyes shut and massaged the bridge of my nose. I wasn't about to argue with him. Tell him how insensitive he was. Or jump on him like I had done hours before.

"I'm giving you an ultimatum." I wiped my face. "Either we get counseling or get divorced. I will never, ever allow this to happen again."

8. COVERING

I was diagnosed with a personality disorder as well as depression and anxiety. And probably a touch of bipolar. I once read an article that proved what I thought all along. That artists, people with the ability to create—writers, singers, dancers, painters—are more susceptible to mental illnesses. I've always been a storyteller, ever since I was six years old. My mind consisted of layers upon layers of imaginative scenarios and characters. Sometimes, I'd stay in those worlds that I created for hours, never coming up for the air, which was what I called "reality." At some points, I'd get trapped in my own mind. Unable to leave or tell what was real. Others would snatch me out, but then I'd be miserable, because in my worlds, I controlled everything. I was the hero. The main attraction. It was safe and clean. People loved me. I was different. I could be whoever I wanted to be.

As I got older, it only got worse. I didn't know how to switch from imagination to reality. So, I masked my confusion of the two with anger. I tried diligently to bridge the gap, but I never could.

"You live in a dream world," hubby told me during my second year of steady therapy appointments.

"I know," I replied, solemnly. "I don't know how to not."

But what he hadn't understood was that the dream world was the glue. If that failed, then all of it failed. And what was left? A carcass, maybe.

"Why do you think you created this make-believe world?" the therapist asked.

I had never told anybody about it, not out loud. It was my little secret. It wasn't for everyone. Just me.

"I never wanted to be me when I was small," I began. "I remember wanting to be adopted. I used to pretend that Mom wasn't my mom at all. I don't think that's normal."

The therapist was quiet, thoughtful for a second. "So, you created these worlds to protect yourself?"

It took a lot not to cry in front of her. Instead, I nodded. "I could be whoever I wanted. Usually the characters were white and heroic. I'd take characters from books and TV shows. That's why I loved adventure books so much. I lived vicariously through them. It sounds weird, but it helped me. Still does."

"It's not helping so much now?"

"There's a disconnect." I shook my head. "But I can't stop it. I don't have anything else to hold onto. If I don't have my worlds, then what do I have? I know I sound crazy. I'm not schizo. I swear."

She let out a small laugh and leaned forward. "You are the patient that I look forward to seeing every week."

I chuckled.

"Imagination is great, but when it starts to become a coping mechanism, a cover to hide what's really going on, then that's when it becomes a problem. You're using this world, these characters, to cope with trauma from your childhood, from your marriage, and I believe there's a better way. We don't have to destroy the whole thing, but if we can, let's try to go a bit deeper."

Although lots of changes were happening with my mental health, I was still very active in the Islamic communities in Detroit, and so were the people close to me. We'd gather up the Muslim girl gang and go to *Jumah* prayer every Friday. It was such a huge deal to dress up, listen to the *khutbah*, and see familiar faces afterward. There'd be a huge bazaar in the common area, where people sold lunches and baked goods and scarves and handmade incense. Little Muslim boys wearing thobes and knitted kufis would run around, chasing one another, weaving in between elders carrying bags of candy.

There was always something to do, always a community event going on to bring everyone together and rejoice in faith. Growing up homeschooled and isolated from our non-Muslim family members, it felt good to finally feel at home. I felt like I belonged to something greater than myself. That was what Islam was all about to me. Community.

Of course, there were certain mosques that I hadn't cared for because the vibes were off. I felt like it was a game of who could walk through the door dressed the holiest, who could arrive the earliest to receive the most blessings. Those types of communities were too harsh, too judgmental for someone like me. I hadn't wanted to cover my face with a black veil or wear gloves or avoid colors. That wasn't the kind of Muslim I wanted to be.

But in any community, any organized religion, there are always issues brewing underneath the surface.

I started to notice the double standards of the men and women. How so much pressure was put on the girls to maintain modesty, be pious and subservient to her husband or the males in her family; it didn't matter the circumstance. They were expected to be understanding and forgiving of a cheating husband or a violent husband. How it was somehow always the woman's fault if a divorce occurred. There was a lot of infidelity happening; Muslim men were having full-blown non-Muslim girlfriends on the side while still being married. And for some reason, many hadn't thought it was an issue to address, that these men were committing the mortal sin of adultery.

But if a Muslim woman entered the mosque with a tight or form-fitting dress on, then the whispers and disapproving eyes would be constant. Some would even be bold enough to confront said Muslim gal to tell her that her dress was inappropriate or that her sleeves were above her elbows and that her prayers wouldn't be accepted because of it. Yes, that actually happened to me.

I internally lost my shit one time, when an imam, in front of the whole congregation, talked about sundresses and how it's distracting for women to wear them in the mosque and that we needed to practice modesty.

The girl in the sundress was me and so many other Muslim girls in the summer. A lot of us are bottom heavy, so whatever we wear, there will be jiggle, and some parts of our womanly forms just can't be hidden. I was literally eye-raped by Muslim men all the time. One in particular was married, and as I stood next to him, he just kept looking me up and down and up and down. I remembered feeling so objectified. So disturbed that we were the ones to blame for men's inability to just look the fuck away and stop being creeps.

What they forgot to add about modesty was that Muslim women and men both needed to observe it. Modesty wasn't just created for women. And that when you do see an indecent person, you lower your gaze. You don't just objectify them, then cry indecency or blame them for your lustful thoughts.

How had Islam become so one-sided? That wasn't the Islam I knew or agreed with.

As time went on, I started to see for myself what my beloved community had come to. How political many of the communities were. How some of them thought they were superior to another because they followed the faith two steps further than the one in the next city. There were scandals and cover-ups and misuse of funds.

There were sexual abuse allegations, from boys and girls. Claims were swept under the rug, and perpetrators free to roam and claim more victims.

I started being less involved.

■   ■   ■   ■

I got a text message: *Imani committed suicide. She shot herself in the head in the basement.*

I put the phone down for a moment, trying to figure out who the sister was.

Which Imani? I texted back.

The one who was always there. Smiling. Her mom used to volunteer in the kitchen.

Still, it didn't click all the way. Her image was at the tip of my memory.

My friend sent me a photo.

Imani was eighteen. She had dark-brown skin, thick brows, and a pretty smile. She looked just like her mama. She was ten years younger than me, so she probably thought of me as an elder or something. I knew her in passing. We always gave a friendly nod and grin, but nothing more. Behind that smile was pain that I could never conceive.

That day, people from the community posted prayers and selfies from Imani's Snapchat in remembrance. They rejoiced in her goodness, her memory. As the hours passed, a glimpse into her life and the event that led her to put a gun to her head began to unravel.

"She was molested for many years," someone revealed. "All her life basically."

A sickness stirred within me, causing my upper lip to twitch as I swallowed back something heavy.

Mom had been molested when she was small. And so had my little sister. My childhood crush was molested by his karate instructor. A friend by her stepfather, who went to prison for it. My ex was touched when he was an adolescent and so was his brother. Some Muslim, some not.

The men that molested Imani were Muslim. There are Muslim men (and women) who are known pedophiles, and they walk among us within the community. It disgusts me to know that these monsters can possibly be praying beside me. How can you call yourself a Muslim and protect a predator? I cannot pray beside a molester. I don't care how close he says he is to God.

Suicide is frowned upon in Islam. In a nutshell, if you take your life, then you go to hell. Although God is also merciful and forgiving, and really no one knows for sure who gets to go to hell or heaven in the end. But I can't stop thinking about it. The process. How can someone like Imani be thrown into the hellfire, punished, when she lived in hell on earth? Those men stole her life before she ever had a chance. God, take them. Snatch their souls from their chests and replace hers with theirs. Theirs are meaningless. What they did, inexcusable.

I began to realize just how much Islam is as confusing to me as it is simple. It may seem cut-and-dried to outsiders, but the mercy is insurmountable. There's a part in the Quran that states if we were to be fairly and equally judged by our sins, then every human being would fill the pits of hell. But because of the forgiveness we receive, we get chance after chance to redeem ourselves. Day after day to do better. Learn more. Inspire more. And for that, I'll never leave the faith.

Hurt people hurt other people. Trauma and illness and abuse surpass faith sometimes. It causes us to do the unthinkable, no matter what religion you follow, no matter what culture you've come from. These kinds of sicknesses don't discriminate.

9. THAT TIME WE WENT TO GUATEMALA

"**I** put your lunch in the bag," I told him as he rushed in and out the room.

"Thanks, bae." He smiled. His one dimple prominent.

"No kiss?" I pouted.

He sighed exaggeratedly and leaned in, pecking me on the lips.

"Wanna do it later?" I raised my brows suggestively.

Giggling like a schoolgirl, he replied, "Yes."

Nine hours later, he'd returned, exhausted as usual. I was still finishing up some blogging work on my laptop when he tossed his shoes by the door and flopped at the edge of the bed. He looked into the dresser's mirror. "Do you love me?"

I grimaced. "What kind of question is that?" I couldn't believe he'd said it. I kept typing because it was the only way to keep me from going off.

"I'm just asking." Passive aggression at its finest, finally earning his graduate-level degree in it. "Cuz if you love someone, you show it."

"I show it all the time when I pack your lunches when I'm busy, when I took care of you when you tore your Achilles' heel, and when your family annoys the fuck out of me. Because it makes you happy, I still go and eat their nasty food. If that's not love, then I don't know what is. You know how I feel about unseasoned veggies from the can."

He shot me a side-eye at the last part.

It was quiet for the next few seconds as he thought about what stupidity he wanted to share next.

"I was talking to this girl at work today. She told me that her man cheated on her, so she cheated back."

"Are these real-life work conversations?" I tried to massage away the irritation forming between my brows.

"Listen," he said. "They are still together. She said that they still love each other."

"That's not love if you have sex with someone else to get back at your spouse. She had revenge sex. She hopped on another dick freely. Not cool."

"I guess." He twiddled his thumbs. "A lot of people at my job cheat."

Now this comment raised my Black-girl spidey senses. I shut my laptop and looked him dead in the face. "So, what you're saying is that you work with a bunch of male whores?"

He crossed him arms over his chest. "Men can't be whores. We were created to spread our seed and multiply."

The conversation was getting worse, and my temperature gauge was cautioning me to abort mission. I said, "The grass isn't always greener on the other side. Cheaters always think that they are leveling up and doing better. They are never true to themselves or others and use sex as validation to fill a void. Most cheaters are insecure as fuck. I'll never respect that shit. And that comment you made about men not being able to be whores is sexist as fuck."

Trying to play it off as a joke by laughing as he usually did, he said, "What would you do if I cheated?"

I took a deep breath, so over the conversation. "Look, I've told you this a thousand times. Don't string me along. Don't embarrass me in front of everyone. If you don't want this anymore, then you don't have to be here. I'll be hurt. I'll be mad. But I'll get over it and find something else."

"Who else would want you?" he asked with a seriousness that I'll never forget.

"Somebody." My jaw clamped. "Maybe."

"Riiiiiight." He rolled his eyes.

"And you're a fuckin' walk in the park. Your head is shaped weird. You leave toenail clippings on the kitchen table and your dick is average." The last comment always made him angry.

He got up. "I'm not talking to you anymore."

"Fine," I said and went back to typing.

■　■　■　■

His work schedule was pretty tight. He'd come home from his job at a stockroom, hop in the shower while I made his lunch, ate, and then went on to his next job at the airport. I felt a pang of guilt that he had to work so hard, so I tried to make sure I had his meals prepped, kept the house cleaned, and argued less.

I mostly knew his work schedule, but on one day, it was off. It was a Thursday. I'd just made him lunch. He brought his food to the couch and got under the blanket.

I looked over suspiciously. "Umm, don't you have to be at work in fifteen minutes?"

He adjusted himself and placed the plate in his lap. No eye contact. "Uhh, I don't have to go in until five."

"That's weird," I said. "Why didn't you tell me?"

"I don't know. Slipped my mind."

"So why five instead of two? Did you switch shifts?"

Still no eye contact. "Nah, I have a staff meeting."

"Oh." I let it go.

After the movie was finished, he got dressed for his "staff meeting." He put cologne on, as he usually did, but he didn't have on his uniform.

"You get to wear regular clothes to work now?" I asked from the couch.

"Yeah, it's a new thing." He kissed me on my forehead, clipped his phone to his belt, and unlocked the door. "We'll do something fun when I get back. Okay?"

"Sure." I nodded, excited that he wanted to take me somewhere instead of watching movies at home all the time.

The following week, his boss called him in early. He took a shower, grabbed his stuff, and raced out the door.

I went to the bathroom to take a poop, and lo and behold, he'd left his cell phone. He neeeever left his phone. I hadn't snooped in years. I thought about driving to his job and dropping it off, but I didn't know what part of the airport he worked in.

Ah well.

I placed the phone on the living-room table and went about my day.

An hour later, he called my cell. "I left my phone. If you need to, you can reach me at this number," he said, with not a waver in his tone.

"I should be okay, but gotcha."

I ended the call and stared at his phone. His notifications from Twitter kept popping up, causing the screen to continuously glow. I picked it up and swiped. There was a code. Now, I knew that he'd put a password on his phone. When I'd asked him about it, he said that he'd placed the lock there just in case someone tried to steal it, along with his information. That was fair. Just to show me that he was trustworthy, he gave me the passcode.

I tried three passcodes, and none of them were correct. It locked me out. See, that's what I got for snooping. A little part of me was worried why he'd changed it, but then I thought there had to be a reasonable explanation.

Feeling in the spirit, I decided to see my friend at Biggby and then head to the grocery store to make hubby a nice dinner. He deserved it.

When I got home, the phone was still blowing up with notifications. Damn, his Twitter was lit. I dropped the grocery bags and picked up the phone. On the screen weren't Twitter notifications; it was missed texts from someone nicknamed Nonie Fly.

I had turned into a straight schizoid. The nickname was of a bitch. I just knew it. But maybe said bitch had the wrong number, or maybe it was a joke, or maybe it was a fuckin' joke.

I tried one, only one, passcode, and the phone magically unlocked. Look at Gawd!

And there it was. Undeniable proof.

I dropped the phone and began to shake. Tears and snot came out of every orifice. How could he? Who was that? Why? How long? Where? My legs couldn't hold my weight, as I tried to stand. I replayed the lines over and over in my head. *I haven't felt this way with nobody, not even my wife. Maybe after we get the physical out, that way we could think better. I have an itch that no one can scratch but u.*

He'd dropped signs, and just like every other woman on the planet, I'd failed to see it before my little feelings got hurt.

I lay back and stared at the ceiling. A cold chill washed over me.

Stop crying, a voice that sounded like mine ordered.

"But I'm hurt," I replied.

You aren't the first woman to get cheated on or the last. Call him. Give him a piece of your mind. Give it to him. He deserves every bit of your wrath.

"But . . ."

Do it.

I regained the strength in my legs. This was where the schizoid part came into play. All the sadness seemed to wash away, the tears dried, and I was no longer hurt by him or this Great Value brand-side piece-work bitch. I was fuckin' furious. I had to stay cool, though, and come up with a plan. Since I'd already gone to jail once for domestic violence, I couldn't touch him or his shit. I had to fuck with his mind instead.

"Hello?" I said to the operator at his job. "Can you tell him to call me when he gets a chance? Thank you so much. Oh, and tell him it's an emergency."

Ten minutes later, he called.

My voice was level. "I want you to listen to me very carefully before responding. This can go really bad or really, really bad depending on your answer. I want you to be truthful and not say any slick shit. Okay?"

"What's going on?"

"Who's Nonie Fly?"

He had the audacity to ask, "Why are you in my phone?"

I laughed. "I guess you ain't hear what the fuck I just said!"

"Calm down."

"I promise you that I will ruin your whole fuckin' life if you don't get yo ass here and start mother-fuckin' talkin'."

"Okay," he said.

I hung up.

Two hours later, he entered the door with an uncomfortable smile. I stood in the kitchen with my arms tightly crossed over my chest and face set.

He approached me. I backed away. "Don't fuckin' come near me."

"Bae, I—"

"Don't say shit," I said and took one look at his lying ass and walked off. I had so much I wanted to say, but I couldn't even get it out. He was a waste of space.

I went to the back room.

He followed, close in pursuit. I dialed the number on his phone.

"What are you doing?"

"Calling the bitch."

"Why does she gotta be a bitch?"

I grabbed a pair of scissors and cornered him. "If you ever in your life stick up for some side BITCH in front of me again, I'll end your shit right here and now."

With fear in his eyes, he nodded.

She didn't answer, so I left a voicemail. "Hey, this is the wife. Yeah, you probably know all about me since you guys had so many amazing conversations about me. I just wanted to let you know that he's now very much so free. So, he's all yours. Have fun. Buh-BYE."

The girl had the audacity to text back saying she made a mistake and that he's a good man and that I shouldn't leave him. Biiiiiitch.

"Just get out," I told him. "I don't want to ever see your face again."

He got on his knees and started crying. "She isn't nobody. That was pillow talk. She's just a ho. She's dated like everybody at work."

I laughed in his face. "So, what does that say about you?"

"I'm sorry," he screamed. "I'm sick in the head. I need help."

"Nah, you just threw away eight years of marriage for some bitch, so go be over there with her."

He pinned me against the wall, putting me in a bear hug. "No, I'm not leaving you."

I tried to fight him, but he had me in a death grip. "I will hurt you, if you don't let me go," I warned. "You are a liar. I will never trust you again."

"She means nothing to me." He let go. "I'll call her right now and call it off."

"Then call her right now," I said.

He was apprehensive, not thinking I'd call him on his bluff. I pulled out the scissors again. He dialed quickly, wiping the tears from his eyes. Of course, she didn't pick up. He left a sad voicemail. "I can't talk to you anymore."

He sounded like some child whose mom made him call his troublesome friend and tell him that they couldn't play anymore.

I was disgusted. And even though he told her that, I still didn't want him.

"I never had sex with her," he said, like that was going to make the situation magically stop.

"I don't trust anything that comes out of your mouth."

"I only went out with her one time to the movies." He lowered his head in disgrace. "I took her that day I told you that I was going to that staff meeting."

"I only have one question," I said. "Does she cover? Does that bitch even wear a hijab?"

Instead, he gave me her life story. "She's Middle Eastern. I thought she could be my second wife, but she said that her family wouldn't accept me."

"I didn't ask for that bitch's life story. Does she wear proper hijab like the one you force me to wear?"

"No."

I got so close to his face, I'm sure spit was flying everywhere as I screamed. "You mean to tell me that you are always telling me how un-Islamic I am, scolding me for wearing tight clothes, calling me a slut. And you cheat on me with someone who doesn't even cover her fuckin' hair?"

"I . . . I," he stuttered.

With my finger in his face, I said, "Don't you ever in your life tell me how I'm not good enough, when you don't even know what the fuck you want."

He slept at his mother's house for two weeks. One of those nights, he slept in a shoddy motel down the street. He told me that a draft came through the windows, causing the room to freeze and that the sheets had cigarette burns in them and that the prostitutes and clients were loud late at night, and that he slept with his gun underneath his pillow. His eyes were bloodshot from crying. He apologized a million times. I felt bad and let him back in the house, but he could only sleep on the lumpy couch. I told him that we needed marriage counseling and that if he ever cheated again, then it was over.

■   ■   ■   ■

Almost a year passed. The marriage counseling had tapered off, and he became the same ole, same ole. I was getting less and less attention from him, but I thought we were just going through a rough patch. The norm was that he came home after work, heated up food that I'd made for him, and plopped down on the couch. I had become just like the couch and the table, a fixture in his world. I wasn't worthy enough for a kiss on the forehead or a hello, how was your day. I was just there as a dumping ground when he wanted sex and a clothes washer and a food maker. But soon things would brighten up, since our anniversary was right around the corner. I was a hopeful, Black housewife.

"Our anniversary is coming up," I reminded him.

"Oh, yeah," he said nonchalantly. "I'm going to Australia."

"But during our anniversary?"

He rolled his eyes. "We aren't like normal people. Society places too much importance on these so-called special days. We can celebrate that anytime."

So, he went on a solo trip to Australia, promising that when he returned, we'd go to Guatemala for our anniversary.

The night before our Guatemala trip, he was being the nastiest human being. Making comments about how I should've been grateful that I had a husband who took me on extravagant trips and that I wouldn't have gone to half the places I've been without him. I retreated to my room and slammed the door. He didn't run after me. A sickness that I'd never felt rose inside my stomach as he packed his luggage just outside that door. I felt like vomiting for absolutely no reason. Then my brother-in-law's voice popped into my head—"He is trying to make you leave him"—something he told me a year earlier when hubby decided to be shady the first time.

"But why?" I'd asked my brother-in-law.

"Because he's not strong enough to let you go. He's going to do all he can to make you hate him until you leave first."

I stood up too fast, my legs almost collapsing from the intensity of every kind of emotion one can carry. I opened the door and went over to him as he stuffed his toothbrush into his backpack.

"If you don't want to be with me, then you don't have to be," I said. "But you won't keep treating me like a nigga on the street. I've put in the work. I've done some fucked-up stuff, but I'm different now. I've gone through therapy to help me handle my anger, but you, you just push and push. You need help. Not me. I'm not the enemy. I'm not your enemy. I'm not."

He looked up at me as if I was speaking in a completely different language and didn't say a word.

■ ■ ■ ■

I always imagined breakups happening like in the movies. Grabs hand. Holds me close. *It's not you . . . I love you but . . . There's someone else . . .*

"I kinda don't want to leave you," hubby told me in the middle of the Delta terminal. "You might be somebody one day."

Wow. What a thing to say after a decade of togetherness.

"I spoke to my mom about it," he admitted. "I wanna do it the right way. You have three months to get your stuff together and move out." Blah. Blah. Blah.

He went on and on about shit that didn't even matter. I zoned out, as tears streamed down my face. I hated crying in public. I hated crying in general. Makes my head hurt and eyes puffy.

Deep down, I knew it was coming. He'd been doing weird shit, and by weird shit, I mean cheating, for the last two years. He'd been putting more effort into the way he dressed, going hard in the gym, vacations to Miami with fuck boys who were known for cheating on every woman they'd ever been with—wives, girlfriends, side-chicks, strippers.

And I chose to think he was . . . different.

"Fuck you." I stood up and began walking away.

"Amerra," he called out.

I stopped. Just like on TV.

Maybe he wanted to recant his statement. Tell me that he was only joking, he didn't want a divorce, let's have hella fun in Guatemala for our eighth-year anniversary as promised. Just maybe we could salvage our relationship.

I looked back at him. Hopeful.

Instead he said, "I'd like you to keep this hush-hush until it's finalized."

God.

Heat washed over me. My nostrils flared, and my heartbeat doubled. I wanted him dead. I wanted to tackle him to the ground and bang his odd-shaped head into the ground. I wanted him to be hurt, humiliated, and scared like I was. He spoke to me like I was a fuckin' nobody. I'd given him a decade of my life, and "hush-hush" was what I was reduced to.

I tore through bodies of travelers waiting to get on their flights, found a restroom, and burst into one of the stalls.

More tears.

Thoughts tumbled over one another, and memories spewed from file cabinets and landed in piles of paper on the floor. We'd been together since we were teenagers. We'd been through shit: meeting my family on my dad's side for the first time, his father's death after he lost his battle with cancer, domestic violence, traveling the world, and the loss of a child. We met each other when he was a little shit. I was far more advanced than he was, but I was also a shit. I was in college. He was just graduating high school. He didn't know how to write a fuckin' check or pay bills. I gave him my car and took the bus to work. I moved to the ghetto so that he could be closer to school, for a degree that he never even finished. I did his résumé, made it look nice and pretty. I forged doctor's notes. I cooked and cleaned. I forgave him when he cheated on me with a bitch from work.

And he had the audacity to leave me? Tell me to keep it hush-hush?

Hurt subsided. For the most part. All that was left was anger. I stepped out the stall and splashed my face with sink water. *Dry those tears.*

I have a tendency to numb myself when shit hits the fan. It's either that or start fucking shit up. And unfortunately, I was Black, Muslim, and at the airport. Not a good idea to start tearing stuff from the walls. I'd be divorced plus in jail.

I returned to the gate and took a seat. All my energy had been drained by a leech of an ex. I slumped my head over and closed my eyes. He sat next to me. I knew it was him because of his scent. I can't describe it, but I was obsessed. I used to smell his pillow when he worked midnights. At night, when he'd fall asleep, I'd dig my face into his neck and just breathe in.

I refused to open my eyes. None of it was real. I wasn't there. Just my body.

He pulled me over. Laid his head on my head. He was never affectionate with me in public. PDA was rare to none. To the people watching, we were a loving couple on our way to Guatemala for our anniversary.

"So, we have to get a divorce for you to be loving?" I asked quietly.

I felt him smile. "Just enjoy the trip."

■　■　■　■

After several missed flights, we finally arrived at the hotel and our room. There were two beds. I guess the universe was cementing our fate in stone.

Jet-lagged, I plopped down on the bed closest to the window. I wasn't sure how to act around him or what to say. In just one moment, he'd become a strange man in my room.

I took a long shower, then hung up my dirty travel clothes over the bathtub. Our luggage had been lost, and who knew when we'd get it back. I exited the bathroom in my undies and bra. Before I could slip under the blankets, he slapped my butt. Like we were together. Like he hadn't just asked for a divorce in the fuckin' airport right before our anniversary vacation.

"Don't ever fuckin' touch me again." I gave him a death stare and covered myself with blankets.

He said nothing. All he did was smile. I had a hard time finding the familiarity in it.

He was the type of guy that masked sadness with grins and uncomfortableness with giggles. He'd always been awkward, but

I liked that about him. I had thought it was charming and sweet. Now, it was condescending and weak.

I faced the window, cocooning myself in those brown blankets. They were my protection from the stranger. Gazing out into the night sky, I was somewhere in the world. Hazy lights lit up the city, as Latin music boomed from a nearby nightclub. I cried silently, trying to keep my sniffles to a minimum, hoping he'd justify them as my usual allergies.

I drifted to sleep, my cheek in a pool of my own excretions.

Hours passed, and I was jolted awake. He had wiggled his way into my bed. My blanket cocoon hadn't done a very good job at protecting me.

"Can I help you?" I asked.

"I know you don't want to be over here all by yourself."

I shook my head. "Get out."

He pulled me over to lay on his chest. He kissed my forehead. I listened to his heartbeats. *Th-thump. Th-thump.* Those heartbeats that didn't belong to me any longer.

He grabbed my face and kissed me. A passion and fire that I hadn't experienced from him in a long time. I pulled away.

"We're getting divorced," I reminded him.

"I know," he said. "But let's just have fun."

He flipped me on my back and gave it to me. And I let him. Like a battered woman. A broken woman without a voice. He'd reduced me to nothingness. Again.

When he finished, I had died. He'd taken any little self-worth I had left and tossed it into the fire.

I hated myself. I hated him.

He fell asleep. I turned over and cocooned myself in the same brown blanket.

We spent the next day shopping for trinkets. Although hurt, I was going to make the most of the trip. I knew that it'd be my last trip for a while, since he was going to cut me off from everything: flight benefits, rent, and health insurance.

Our last stop was dinner at the Hard Rock Café.

"Having fun?" he asked sitting across from me in a booth.

I looked up from the menu and mustered a smile. "Yep."

We placed our orders. I watched the music videos behind his head when he started talking about the divorce. Yet again. As if I hadn't heard the first time.

"I just feel like I was never a priority for you," he began.

"Hey!" I shouted. "We've talked about this before. Can we talk about something else? At least until we get back home."

He continued, "You never gave me sex when I wanted, and you were always hanging out with your friends late at night. I just think we've grown apart. But you'll always be my first love."

I lifted my eyes to the sky to keep them from watering.

"I mean, I don't think you want to be with me anyway."

I slammed my fist on the table. "Are you kidding me? I cook and clean for you. I make sure my shit is taken care of. I don't ask you for shit. Who the hell took care of you when you got hurt playing basketball? Are you serious?"

"Calm down," he said.

"C-calm down?" I waved the waiter over and pointed to a colorful mixed drink. I knew that'd make him mad. He hated when I drank liquor. "Two." Both were for me.

The waiter brought one. I downed it. The only way I was going to get through the rest of the trip was to drown myself in vodka.

"You know what," he said. "I wish I could just take your pussy off your body and leave the rest behind."

I would consider myself hard on the exterior, able to take a punch, a joke, a mean comment. But that . . . it knocked the wind from my lungs, it slithered around me and constricted, it reduced me to dust. All I was to him was pussy? Was that all I ever was? Was that what all women were to men? A huge sexual organ?

What had I done to him to make him hate me so much? I mean, I knew in the beginning I wasn't the best wife, person, but I had gone to therapy. I'd gotten better. I wasn't cured of all my bad habits, but I was getting better.

That ugly cry, the one that resembled the face of a crocodile trying to smile. The kind of cry that stuck in your throat and caused you to hyperventilate. The kind that waited for that moment of complete humiliation, hurt, and trauma spanning from years and years ago and carried with you up until now. That's how I cried.

He rushed to my side and tried consoling me. I pushed him. He tried it again and again, until I allowed him to soothe me. He always cared so much about what people thought of him. Now he looked like the spouse of the year to the non-English-speaking waitresses behind the bar.

"It's okay. You're going to have a good life without me. You're strong and smart. It's just not working with me and you anymore," he said. As he droned on, trying to make himself feel better more so than me, I eyed the butter knife. I went through a scenario of stabbing him in the arm, neck, wherever with it. It wouldn't kill him, but at least he'd shut the fuck up.

On the last day, we decided to sightsee. We had no idea where we were going, and the taxi driver didn't speak English. And what was worse than getting lost in the mountains? Getting lost in the mountains with your emotionally abusive ex. The taxi driver took us to this small city forty-five minutes away.

The roads were paved with spaced-out, chunky bricks. Immediately, I saw a bunch of white people and knew we had hit the tourist spot. The city had a rustic charm. Huge churches were on every corner and little street carts selling fresh pineapple juices. Inside the city's square was a park with a waterfall. Guatemalan women and little girls surrounded it with colorful native dresses and braided pigtails. They were trying to sell cheap toys to the visitors.

We took lots of photos. None together.

He was walking in front of me, and I saw a little girl wrapped on her mother's back as she carried all these colorful stick toys. I snapped a photo. In the corner of it was part of his back and his arm.

We hailed a taxi and headed back to the hotel to pack. This driver was more dangerous than the first one. As he drove on the tails of other drivers, I searched through the photos I'd just taken.

He looked over my shoulder.

Annoyed, I gave him a side-eye.

"When you're done, can I see the pictures of me?"

I shrugged then passed him the camera. *My* camera. The one I'd bought with *my* own money.

He clicked back and forth, deleting the photos of himself that he didn't like.

It was hard not to roll my eyes to the back of my head. I just wanted him to give me the camera back.

Finally, he passed it to me. I went back through the photos again. I wanted to send him his individual photos ASAP, so I could delete them all immediately. Delete like I wanted him to be from my life.

I clicked through and noticed the one with the girl tied to her mom's back was missing. I went back and forth frantically. "Where is that one photo of the girl?"

"I deleted that one," he said nonchalantly.

"That wasn't even a photo of you." My voice started to rise. "Your arm was in it. Your back was turned. I could've cropped you out!"

"My bad." He turned to face the window.

"My bad? My fuckin' bad?"

He faced me again. "You're making a scene."

Five years of extensive therapy went out that window and into that fresh Guatemalan air. It went up to the sun, and with a *hiss* that bitch burned to a crisp. And I'm not sure if I was genuinely mad about the photo being deleted or if that was the last granule that hit the bottom of the hourglass.

"That's your fuckin' problem. You do what *you* want to do. Fuck everyone else. Shit on their feelings." My hands flailed in the air. "As long as you are good, then the fuckin' world is great. You are the most selfish, condescending, sexist, fucked-up human being that I ever met. And I'm sooooo glad that we're getting divorced. This is the best fuckin' thing that's happened to me in a long time. I don't have to see your stupid, ugly-ass siblings, pretend to eat their nasty-ass food, or converse with your ghetto-ass family. Fuck you. *Fuck* them. And don't ever in your life think that you can delete any of my fuckin' photos."

The taxi driver never looked back, never spoke a word. He just continued driving crazy as ever, as the Black couple in the back went ham on each other.

■   ■   ■   ■

In Islam, during a divorce, a man is obligated to take care of his wife for three menstrual cycles (about three months) to make sure she's not pregnant. It also allows time for reconciliation and so the woman can get back on her feet: find a job, housing, etc.

He thought he was being gracious by allowing me to stay in the apartment, and he never forgot to remind me of how grateful I should've been, especially when other men he knew personally would've kicked me to the curb. Although he paid the bills, the apartment was in both our names, but he still asserted his last bits of power over me during those last months.

We were sleeping separately, like roommates, but that didn't stop him from barging in my room and requesting that I have sex with him or make lunch or wash a load of work clothes.

"We aren't together anymore," I told him, peering from behind my laptop.

"So what?" he said.

I giggled. "Why don't you have that bitch you cheated on me with make you a sandwich?"

"You're still in my house." He pointed in my face. "Remember that."

"Fine." I laid the laptop down, hopped out of bed, and retreated to the kitchen like the maid I was.

It was demeaning, but what other choice did I have? I couldn't stay with anyone else. No one had room for me and my stuff. My older sister had offered, but they were already packed into a small apartment. So, I chose space over dignity. Over and over again in my head, I'd repeat: This. Is. Only. Temporary.

Some days when he'd lounge on the couch and talk to other girls right in front of me, I'd want to hurt him. I'd be cleaning the mess he made in the kitchen or making dinner for him, and he didn't even have the decency to phone in the car or at work or his mom's house.

One time, I was making spaghetti. I cut up bell peppers with a long sharp knife. He chatted it up with some girl. The light gleamed off the blade as I held it up. So sharp. Sharp enough to cut through skin, muscle, and organs. I took the knife and held it to my side and clutched the handle. The grease in the pan popped and sizzled. The pace of my breathing quickened, and my heart *th-thumped* against my rib cage. I plunged the knife tip first into the bell pepper and cut the pieces finely.

My ex and his two friends helped me move the large pieces of furniture into my new place with my roommate. I was stressed because I didn't have the money to pay for a truck or movers. And he and his crew were the only people I could get to help me on a weekday. For sure, he was going to know exactly where I was going to be and who I was going to live with. I was livid.

He backed the U-Haul into the driveway, then hopped out. His friends followed. When they opened the back door, shit started to fall out. My shit. They had lazily stacked furniture and boxes like the amateurs they were, even though I told them to not overpack the truck. But what had I known? I was just a newly divorced female living on her own.

"Nice place," he said, surveying the manicured lawn and newly surfaced siding.

The stuff that they hadn't broken, they brought upstairs to my area. Luckily, they only had three things to carry, so they'd be in and out in less than twenty minutes.

"Well, thanks for everything. Bye!" I said. He took it upon himself to look around. I stood there with annoyance plastered on my face. "Seriously?"

"So, who are you renting from?"

"A man," I said.

He turned around quickly. "What Muslim woman lives with a man?"

I rolled my eyes until they couldn't roll back any further. "He's gay."

He scoffed, "That's even worse."

"You're such a piece of fuckin' work," I said. "The guy that I'm rooming with is very nice, he works with children, he's traveled the world, and he's made me feel very, very comfortable. His house is clean, and he treats me with decency. No, he's not Muslim and certainly doesn't like vagina, but what's it to you? You think you're better? Well, let me remind you how fucked up you are. You just ended a ten-year relationship because you couldn't keep your dick in your pants. Your sisters are running around these streets with other people's husband's cocks in their mouths and your brother is in and out of jail. And your other sister can't keep her legs closed. So, I'm really confused as to why you are throwing the first fuckin' stone?"

His mouth gaped open as he hovered over me, at a loss for words.

I raised an eyebrow. He stormed out. And then I locked the door behind him.

■ ■ ■ ■

When I was born, there was a mustard seed of an Angry Black Bitch buried inside. How life affected me dictated how it grew. Less stress and trauma meant that it stayed small, manageable. More negative impact allowed it to sprout and twist about like a vine around my heart and brain, suffocating it like a pillow to a face.

Seeing Mom beat down by my brother's father. Witnessing Mom being handcuffed in front of a drugstore because she was stealing diaper rash ointment for my baby brother. The faint memory of being placed in the back seat of that patrol car. Lying on my back upstairs listening to her argue with my father about his absence. Being asked if I was a boy because I was fat and Mom dressed me in shapeless clothing. Having an abortion at nineteen. Cutting off my nappy hair, hoping it'd grow back more luxurious than ever. Being arrested for domestic violence. Barely graduating from college. Being racially profiled. Discriminated against because of my religion. Losing weight, just to gain it all back plus some. Divorcing after almost a decade. Being cheated on. Tossed to the side like I ain't shit. Taken for granted. Used and abused.

At first the Angry Black Bitch festered in her newfound host, but I was strong enough—or fake enough—to keep her at bay. Wouldn't want hubby to think I wasn't subservient enough. That I, in fact, had my own feminist views that trumped whatever sexist foolishness he stood by. That I was able to overpower him intellectually or financially or in any other emasculating way. That I was a safe housewife, only there to serve and nothing more.

Wouldn't want Mom to think that I was falling into the same traps as she had growing up. That I, too, was on the verge of becoming a statistic. A struggling, single parent whose life wasn't hers anymore but belonged to a snot-nosed child that sucked up any remaining creative energy I had and a baby daddy that wasn't shit.

And, of course, we wouldn't want the community to know that I wasn't praying as I should have, as a God-fearing Muslim should have. Wouldn't want to be seen as a bad Muslim girl.

It was much safer to keep all of that to myself.

But Angry Black Bitch wanted out.

There was a smile in her voice as she went on a rampage. *Say what the fuck you want when you want. Be raw. Be fearless. Unapologetic. Walk with your head high. Buy a fur coat and wear that bitch to the grocery store. Be extra. Extra as fuck. When white people are uncomfortable, make 'em more uncomfortable. Don't protect their feelings. Ever. And do the same with Black people too. Black men will stick up for non-Black women. Call them out. Hit 'em with that Black girl magic. Same for Islamophobes. Fuck them especially. Most of them are stupid as fuck anyway. It's easy to shut they asses down. And you know you have those Muslims who are straight haters. You know the ones I'm talking about. The ones who got so much shit to say about what you're doing ain't enough. How less of a Muslim you are because you wear makeup and nail polish. The hypocritical ones that sit there and hide behind religion, even though they have black hearts. Always clap back on them.*

After the pep talk Angry Black Bitch and I had when I invited her in, I was left empowered. Before that, people had talked to me any kind of way, embarrassed me in front of others. Made me feel like I needed their validation in order to thrive. When the only validation I ever needed was from myself. I had made it to another level of consciousness after my divorce. I wasn't sure if I was woke or not, but it sure as hell felt like it.

Angry Black bitch encouraged me to know when to pick and choose my battles. To speak up. To protect my sisters. To celebrate my body. My accomplishments. To say fuck no. To step out of my comfort zone and fuckin' live a little.

She gave me hope when my marriage went down in flames. Power to be like, it's okay to be single. That being in a relationship wasn't going to make or break me. To shut down racists and sexists and bigots. To yell as loud as they had. Be passionate. Fearless. Vulnerable. Cute. Ugly. Fat as fuck. Dope as fuck. Cuss. Pretend to be Sailor Moon. Have a hangover. Recoup from a hangover. Wear nail polish. Put a middle finger up. Smile. Cry. Be a friend.

I learned in the process that there was nothing wrong with having a little Angry Black Bitch speak her peace every now and again.

And that it was time to start writing a new chapter.

PART 4
BUSTING OUT

10. REBEL WITH A HIJAB

It was 4 a.m. I sat at the edge of a bed that wasn't mine. I was surprised that I was awake, scribbling away as the small, mounted LG TV played a French version of America's *CSI* drama series. The foreign words formed long lines of sentences that I didn't even try to grasp. Thank God, I felt a little less jet-lagged. My American body was still readjusting to the five-hour time difference. I found myself sleeping in segments, every two hours like an infant. I got up to pee and flop my fat ass on the small and very low toilets of Europe. A lot of warm pee splashed into the bowl. I complained to myself about how cold it was and massaged the sleep from the corners of my eyes before I wiped my cooch. Then I hopped back into bed and cocooned myself in the blankets.

The day before was rough. Eventful but rough. I had managed to fly to Europe on some *Eat Pray Love*–type mission after my divorce that included living out my Instagram model dreams and booked an in-studio photo shoot with a UK-based retailer. Before the shoot, I had gotten lost for forty-five minutes. Sauntering up and down the street like a turtle on steroids with a heavy-ass backpack weighed down by two pairs of shoes, scarves, and outfits. Ya know, just in case. I might've been from Detroit, but I was professional and prepared to slay. I gave up and hailed a cab. Hailing cabs in the UK was different from the US. They didn't stop in the "red zones" of the streets. Flustered, I asked an English woman smoking a cig, "Do you guys hail cabs differently here?" She smiled and politely told me the "rule." I thanked her and tried to find a non-red zone area.

I finally found the office. It was fancy. I wore my "Black Lives Matter" sweater and felt out of place. The receptionist, who was of color, shot me a disapproving look, then notified the team that I had arrived. Two very white Londoners wearing chic ensembles held their hands out, clearly expecting to shake hands. Instead, I gave them a double hug. They giggled and led me to the sixth floor. I got to meet the head of the department. They brought me tea and water and had an entire setup of shoes and clothes and a backdrop and an expensive-looking camera. We knocked out four outfits and two videos.

And then I was on to the next shoot! I felt like a fat-ass Naomi Campbell.

I hadn't set out to become a model. I was just an on and off blogger, taking pics of my clothes and styling other people for free. I started a blog twice in the early 2000s. They were both ridiculous and sloppy, and I failed miserably until the third stint of a blog ended up sticking and resonating with audiences in 2013.

Obviously, I enjoyed abuse.

There were a few reasons why I kept trying to make the blogging thing work: People kept mistaking me for a model or a fashion designer when I'd go to events in Detroit. I also had my master's degree in creative writing and wanted to put the eighty-thousand-dollar out-of-pocket education and skills to use. But mostly I was bored after being injured at work (a patient attacked me causing me to fall over a chair and injure my knee very badly leaving me barely able to walk), so I thought, "I have no job and unlimited time, so why not start yet another blog?"

One morning, I woke up and the sun was shining brightly in my face. I scrolled on Instagram and saw a photo of Essie Golden, a fat babe and integral part of the plus-size blogging community. She had big boobs and big hips and fierceness to match. I could do it too, I thought. Seconds later, the name *Beauty and the Muse* popped into my head. The name was the epitome of who I was. There was *beauty* in myself, inward and outward, but I was also a *muse*, a deep thinker. I had no idea what I was doing, but with a grainy Android phone and some wild outfits, I published my first blog post—and third attempt—on May 2013.

I set up two photo shoots. The first one was supposed to be colorful, and the second, dark and high fashion. Although I did the shoots, I hated how I looked in both. I kept asking myself, as the photographer flipped through the raw images, is that how I really looked? Are those really my double chins?

I was just too self-conscious about my body. I wasn't ready to see myself, and I wasn't ready for others to see a body that I wasn't proud of. I decided to stop modeling and focus on highlighting fashion events and becoming a stylist for straight-size models.

I remember being the girl that stood hidden behind the black curtain waiting for skinny models to toss their garments to me after ripping the runway. I was surrounded by women who were confident enough to prance around in thongs awaiting the designer to dress them. If only I was tall and weighed 120 pounds. Then I could be living the life too.

I didn't fit those beauty standards. So I removed any ideas of ever being a model.

My blog baby turned a year old, and my friend Ramona, who owned a vintage clothing store, asked me to come to her store to wrap turbans for her models. When I arrived, I asked her which models she was using.

"What models?" she replied. "You are the model."

I rolled my eyes. I had let that dream go. Why couldn't she?

She wrapped me in African cloth and added vintage pieces to it. I stood stiff, nervous about how my fat body looked. She handed me a black party dress and held it up to my chest. "This should fit," she gushed.

I went to the bathroom and slipped it on. It wouldn't zip up in the back.

I was so used to the walk of shame outside of a dressing room, the shame of something not fitting.

She tried her best to zip it, but my upper body was just too big. "No worries," she said. "We'll just shoot it from the front."

I wanted to be a good sport, so I agreed. I wasn't comfortable. In the dress. In my body. But I wanted them to have some good shots. I didn't want them to feel as though they wasted their time on a fat girl. So I sucked up all of my insecurities for the moment and harnessed characteristics becoming of a queen. If I could pretend to be confident, feel pretty enough, then maybe it'd stick.

When she sent me the photos the next day, something clicked. I was the biggest that I'd ever been, but those photos were so beautiful and so gritty. It was like seeing myself for the first time in years. I'd been so conditioned to feel ugly that I had forgotten that there is beauty in the human body, my body.

I posted the photos to Instagram with a caption about how, during that shoot, I struggled to find beauty in my body. People from all over the world began sending me messages and commenting about their very struggle with body image. The photos got so much attention. And I was only being myself, being transparent.

After those photos, I had photographers reaching out to me to model for them.

Not only had I inadvertently become a social media influencer but a model too. I became addicted to Instagram, researching all the plus-size-model hashtags, wanting to know all the pioneer plus-size models that came before me. I found a few, but the one that stuck out was Velvet D'Amour.

I wrote an article about her on my blog, then sent it to her. Weeks later, she actually read it and responded. I melted. An icon was talking to MEEEEEEE!

Months later, she followed me on Instagram. She'd like photos here and there. Then she added me on Facebook. I died, then was resurrected. She said on one of her posts that she was looking to do photo shoots of models in New York. I was in Detroit and didn't have the money to travel. I was devastated, but I always knew that one day the universe would conspire so that I could shoot with her.

And it had. Six months after my divorce, a lump sum of fifteen thousand dollars was awarded to me after fighting a worker's comp case for almost two years for my injured knee.

That was my cue from the universe to hop on a plane and explore what life is, what it could be.

I chose London as my destination.

■　■　■　■

I hopped on the Tube and trekked through rain until I came to a set of yellow doors. I entered, spoke to the very posh receptionist/gatekeeper at her Ginger Spice desk. She told me to enter the café area. The two-person team lounged on the couch and stood when I walked up. The photographer had a fiery red beard and hair. Through his English accent, there was a softness in his tone. I was in love already. The stylist led me to her third-floor office, where I ripped open brand-new clothes ordered specially for me.

"Be you," the stylist said. "It's your style that we want to showcase."

Could definitely fuck with that mentality, I thought. We bumped out five complete looks. Afterward, they took me out for fancy cake and ginger beer, and we chatted about "boning" and my inability to flirt or tell guys that I liked them.

I was learning so much in Europe.

After that, I hopped on the Tube and got ready for a dinner meeting with an editor of a magazine. We chatted over lamb and hummus till about elevenish. I didn't get back until late, and at that moment, I knew that I had fucked up. I had to be up at four in the morning to catch an Uber to the station where I'd take a forty-five-minute train ride to the airport in order to catch a plane to be at a shoot for the great Velvet D'Amour in Paris.

I wasn't even packed.

I absolutely could not fuck up the opportunity. She was an international photographer, walked in Jean Paul Gaultier's show in Paris, walked for John Galliano, and was featured in *Vogue*. She was an icon. The first of her kind. I'd been following her for years. I couldn't fuck this up.

After I packed, I didn't get in bed for another two hours. Four a.m. came like two minutes later. Hit me like a tsunami and took me under the current. I sat there with braids on my head pointed every which way and stared at the eggshell-colored wall. Why had I stayed out so late the night before? And how was I going to give Velvet 110 percent if I was dead? Because that's what I was, dead. A Walker. My feet dangled over the side, as I flexed my swollen ankles. They were sore, too, from all the walking, and the thousands of stairs I had climbed the day before. I never wanted to see a fuckin' stair in my life after that. Flat plains only.

I finally stood and almost fell back down. My knees. My back. That damn heavy-ass backpack I lugged around the London streets. On top of that, I had a dry cough that I couldn't shake, like I had smoked packs of cigars for the last twenty years. Bags circled my eyes.

Hobbling to the bathroom, I washed my face and hit the hot spots with a rag filled with holes. Every movement was painful. How the fuck was I going to make it through travel and a full day? Impossible! I looked in the mirror and thought about my divorce and how this trip was to test my endurance. See what I was really made of. Slow and steady, I said and nodded.

I took the smallest steps as I packed up and wafted out of the hotel and toward the station, and into the train. My eyes kept rolling back in my head, as I feared that my purse would get stolen as I snored. The combination of the darkness of the tunnels and the hum of the car on the tracks became a monotonous lullaby.

"Gare du Nord," the French-voiced system announced. I looped my arm through the thirty-pound pack and hoisted it painfully on my already-sore back. *Slow and steady.* Travelers nearly ran me over as they tried to make it off the platform with heavy rolling luggage. I mean, I wanted to move faster, but my bones said, *Nah, you good.* With each tiny step, I hurt. But I kept going.

I asked for directions at least five times. One guy guffawed as I spoke to him. Angered by his French attitude, I walked away.

I found a Black woman with only a slight accent who gave me thorough directions, which I was grateful for. Black girl magic existed in Paris too.

An hour later, I took a bus to another hotel where we were shooting. The Middle Eastern driver stopped and, before I got off, said, "Be careful around this area. Pickpockets."

I nodded. "I've been told."

I'd been forewarned about the Parisian pocket slicers. They were coming for wallets and passports of all shapes and sizes, and I wasn't going to be a victim. I clutched my purse to my chest and rushed through the crowd. It was a mad house. Worse than New York during rush hour. I made a sharp right and entered the Angleterre Hotel.

I'd made it with my slow and painfully steady pace. I had one foot in the door and one out, when a car honked. I looked over my shoulder, and there was a wild-haired blonde with her head stuck out the window, waving. "Heeeeeeeey!"

It was none other than the coveted Velvet D'Amour. The woman who paved the way for other plus-size women in the fashion industry like Tess Holliday and Ashley Graham. She'd done Cannes for goodness' sake!

Her friend Janet, an Assyrian with wavy hair and blue eyes, hopped out of the car and walked over toward me with a warm smile. "Hello, welcome to Paris," she gushed and kissed me on both cheeks.

Then Velvet came over. The icon stood in front of me. I played it cool. Her hair was different shades of blonde with grayish roots that blended naturally. Her lips were lined with bubblegum-pink gloss. She was a drag queen in a woman's body. We hugged. She was soft. "I know your IG name: LVernon2000," she admitted. "What's your real name? Samantha?"

I laughed. "No. People call me Leah V or LV. Sounds like a superhero name. Right?"

"It does!" she yelled.

She carried huge bags and a briefcase to the elevator. "Okay, you two get in," she ordered.

Janet got in with her suitcase. I looked at the tiny box. "What the hell?"

"Welcome to Paris, where everything is tiny."

The elevator literally could fit one person in it. A claustrophobe's nightmare. Not wanting to seem too American, I held my backpack and squeezed in. Uncomfortably close to the Assyrian beauty, up we went to the second floor. The room was modest. No frills, but comfortable, compact, very Parisian. The twenty-four-hour journey would surely turn me into a Parisian bombshell in no time, accent and all.

Velvet entered and started pulling tutus and lingerie out of bags, as the makeup artist set up her station. "Do your blogger thing and put some outfits together." Her blue eyes were big.

I picked up mesh tops and neon body-con dresses and placed them against my chest. She grabbed one size-small-looking dress and tossed it. I caught it and took my sweater off, exposing my ugly Walmart sports bra that had seen its better days, near a window that was wide open. She noticed my apprehension and waved. "It's only a department store across the street."

"Yes, I'm sure they've seen many fat bodies through the window before." I slipped the dress over my head, and it stopped right at my hips. A normal issue for my big booty self. Janet saw my struggle and pulled the tight fabric over my wide hips until the high slit was prominent. I looked like an overweight version of the redhead from *Who Framed Roger Rabbit*.

"Ohhh, look at that *booty*! Can't wait to exploit it."

I scoffed, "I don't do butt shots."

Velvet got thoughtful, as she lay across the bed like a goddamn queen. "I noticed from your Instagram that you don't show your butt. I never even knew you had one."

I giggled. "That's intentional."

"Wait." She paused. "Your booty doesn't make you feel powerful?"

The question was legit. Sometimes I was embarrassed by its width and height. Always bumping into shit. I've knocked over so many glasses of water trying to squeeze by. Guys objectified me for it. Obsessed over it. Overlooked my education and wit. My ass and I had a love-hate relationship.

"I guess," I replied.

"Girl, there is power in that ass. Do you want to find a good-looking husband? You'll find one for sure in that dress."

Glancing at Janet, I said, "Your friend is crazy."

She laughed, lining up her lipsticks. "I know."

I slipped out of the dress. "It's too tight."

"I know. It's my prostitute dress. That's why God made me fat. If I was skinny, I'd probably be a street girl." She flipped her hair.

"Ohmigod," I replied and picked up a pair of shiny spandex leggings. "Ohh, these are cute. Could definitely rock these." I placed a pair of feather-and-tulle-lined shoulder pads on my shoulders and paraded around.

"Fancy," she gushed.

I tried on another outfit, a golden body-con dress with poofy shoulders. "The waist and booty are too much for me." I shook my head. "What's your obsession with butts?"

"Look." She eyed me. "You want more followers, then I'm gonna need you to show more ass. Okay? It's a thing now, and hell, it'll probably always be a thing. Curvy butts and hips are feminine. Show that ass!" Then she said, "Truthfully, I want you to be comfortable. I know you're Muslim and all. I wouldn't exploit my models."

"I don't doubt that," I said sarcastically. "But for you, I'll show a little butt. I trust you won't make me look raunchy."

She nodded like a person who would definitely exploit someone's hidden raunchiness.

I'm very picky about my makeup, but Velvet assured me that Janet was the best at what she did. Still, a white woman matching my caramel skin tone? Unheard of. I didn't want to be "that" person, so I sat down and allowed her to do her thing. As she blotted my face with a makeup wipe, I confessed, "Never had a white girl do my makeup before." I ended with a nervous chuckle.

She paused. "I'm Chaldean."

"Oh." I thought all about the stores Chaldeans owned in the city of Detroit. "They are pretty racist where I'm from."

She frowned, then shot me a surprised look. "Really?"

I nodded solemnly.

In her French accent, she said, "I'm going to tell my mom this."

I felt bad.

But then she told me, "I'll also tell her about the famous Black, Muslim model that I've met too."

I felt a little better.

She lined my lid with red and green liner, and the false lashes were the final touch. Everyone knew that I loved lashes, since mine were barely there. Falsies took me from a six to a clean eleven, and I was ready for my first editorial shoot in Par-ee (rolls tongue).

The daylight was dwindling, and the sunlight wasn't on our side. I followed Velvet to the tiny-ass Parisian elevator, and together we squeezed in, fat belly to fat belly. Her black camera lay on her chest. She dug in her bra and adjusted her boobs. "I hate underwires," she complained.

I perked my boobs up through my leotard and winked. "Thanks for the faux boobies."

Earlier she had listened to me complain about not having breasts, dug in hers, and pulled out a pair of fake ones, saying, "Drag queens give me so many ideas. Gotta' love em."

When the lift stopped, we stepped out and rounded the corner, where tourist pamphlets occupied the corner wall. We passed the front attendant, nonchalantly leaning back in a chair behind the desk. He said something to Velvet in French. I assumed he wanted to know about the fashionably clad American and the big camera. She responded, "Mannequin."

He nodded and we exited.

"Mannequin?" I asked.

"Yes, model." She crossed the street.

I was a mannequin! Sounded much fancier when Parisians said it.

"Now go stand against that wall and don't be a blogger."

Her complete sass was something I aspired to have each and every damn day.

In the first outfit, I appeared to be a high-fashion superhero. I wore a body suit, a netted cape, and a turban. I stood in the middle of the street that smelled of sewage and fast-food.

From behind the camera, she yelled, "I need you to be a superhero. Try jumping."

As a fat girl, there was only so much air time I was able to achieve, but I was down for the challenge. I got maybe three inches off the ground. It was hard posing and jumping. Who'd I think I was, Coco Rocha?

After she took a few shots, I asked, "Am I ugly? I feel ugly."

She flipped through a few pics. "Eh. Nope."

"Good enough." I hunched my shoulders.

With every outfit change, the antics got wilder, and so did the patrons watching us—me. Now mind you, in America I had done plenty of street shoots and shoots in public places. I've had people point and laugh, look at me as if I was a unicorn. I've had people give compliments and even sneak in a photo. A few will quietly watch. But Parisians took the cake of passerby extra-ness. When I tell you that they were wild and rowdy, that's an understatement.

My face was beat. Lashes on fleek. My broke ass got to Paris, so I was gonna go all out with my ensembles. For the second outfit, I wore a pair of silver, sparkly hot pants that pulled up to mid-waist. I'd been in the gym, and although still very fat, the waist was semi-snatched, and I wanted to accentuate that. I wore a bodysuit underneath that. Janet pinned outrageous and Gaga-esque feather shoulder adornments on me. I slipped on pointy silver metallic shoes and kept the turban chic.

As soon as I stepped on the pavement, a group of men paused, eyes widened, as I approached Velvet.

"Ready to snatch a man?" She grinned.

"Of course." I pouted and lifted my chin.

She pointed. "I need you to sashay very exaggeratedly toward me and spin. Very *Vogue* and confident."

My hips were ginormous, and my butt moved to its own personal drumbeats. I posed and placed my hands on my waist. Very Tyra-like. I walked. A shoulder back, arch in the curve, stomach flat, sway and sashay glide. As Velvet clicked, I spun, danced, and flirted with the lens. The men in the street, of every race from African to Middle Eastern to European, whistled, pointed, and spoke among themselves. I heard one boldly yell, "Big Booty. Big Booty!" Anything in French sounds much nicer. There were lots of "ohmigods." Some blew me kisses. Others kissed their own fingers and loudly expressed their *muahs* (air kisses). "Bee-you-ti-ful," one said in broken English.

"They're just loving all over you," Velvet laughed.

I wasn't sure how to feel. The situation was out of my element. So, I just smiled really hard at the very persistent ones.

"They are going to want to take photos with you next," she warned.

"Oh."

And sure enough, men started pulling out their phones, taking selfies with me and asking their friends to snap photos. Velvet did her best to shoo them away, but they weren't taking no for an answer. On guy in particular was very excited, awe filling his eyes.

"French?" He inquired.

I shook my head. "American."

"Ohhhh." He followed that with, "Telephone?"

"No. No international calling." I hunched my shoulders.

He wasn't giving up. "Facebook?"

His persistence surpassed the others. It was slightly endearing. "Sure," I said.

Velvet wanted me in the middle of rush-hour traffic.

"Now turn to the side and show me some booty."

I rolled my eyes. There were ten times as many men and women trying to cross the street, dodge traffic, and hop on the subway. Plus, if I tooted my booty, I'd get all the bad attention. I angled my body a little, still hiding the curve of my rump.

"Turn more," she said.

I turned a little more.

"More!"

I sighed. It was now or never. I hadn't come to Paris to play it safe by any means. The point of the trip, the shoot, was to dive in. Yes, there were about a hundred people watching me, but I was like a mini-star, so I might as well soak that shit up.

I turned all the way, arched my back for more butt camera action. She snapped rapidly. The crowd across the street waiting for the light to turn green began to whistle and clap. I posed more, Velvet cheering me on from behind the lens. Then, I looked over at the men and women bunched together and smiled. They went full on crazy with roars and applause. You would've thought I was Rihanna or something stepping off a plane. I hardly ever blush, but that was funny to me, endearing. Surreal. My fat body was something to be celebrated, instead of ashamed of.

I thought back to a time when taking a risqué photo in a tight outfit would've resulted in a cuss out by my ex, in body shaming. On our Islamic holiday, Eid, I always wore dresses to the prayer and festivities. One year I wanted to try something different. I was going to rock a pantsuit with a blazer. I had found the shirt and satin blazer the week before and had tried desperately to find the perfect pair of slacks that were loose and modest. I'd gone to at least seven stores. Eid was the next morning, so I had to settle on a pair of slacks that were tight. I knew that hubby would be a bit annoyed, but maybe I could get away with it.

I stepped into the mosque, feeling good and looking great. All the sisters stopped me and looked me up and down. "What a fashionista!" they exclaimed and showered me with kisses and hugs. We took selfies and tons of group photos. A seemingly happy occasion until I saw Hubby standing with his family. I made my way across the room and tried to hug him. He didn't hug me back.

"What's wrong?" I asked.

"Why are you wearing pants?"

I scoffed, "What? I can't wear pants now?"

"They are tight."

"My shirt is long," I replied.

"Everyone can see your shape. Do you see all these men here looking at my wife?"

I grabbed his arm. "No one is looking."

He snatched his arm away and left me standing. I grinned nervously as his hatin' ass sisters frowned at me from their cave—I mean table.

Later on, I tried to make things better, but then he blew up in the car. "Who comes out the house looking like that?" he yelled, darts of spit flying from his mouth. "You couldn't have put on a dress? You embarrassed me."

I sunk further down into the seat, crying. "I just wanted to wear a pantsuit this time."

"They don't sell looser pants?!"

"Do you have to scream?" I sat up. "And no, I went to so many stores, and this was what could fit."

By the next Eid, I had learned my lesson. I used my own money to get a dress made, since I had embarrassed him so bad and he made me feel like I just had walked in front of his family in a bikini. The dress was long-sleeved, fitted at the top with a full swing skirt at the bottom. It was a little big in the waist, so I had the seamstress make a matching belt.

Once again, I walked to the mosque and was greeted by the sisters who swooned over my custom-made dress. Hubby was on his phone, leaning against the wall. I snuck in behind him. He looked up and grinned. I twirled then posed. "How do you like my dress?"

He looked me up and down, then said, "It's too tight in the waist, and I can still see your shape."

Damned if I do, and damned if I don't. There was no pleasing him. No matter how I chose to adorn my curves, he'd never be satisfied. Looking back, this whole tight-clothes-versus-loose-clothes debate got me thinking. No matter what I chose to wear, someone out there would criticize it. Loathe it. Tell me that I could do better.

I figured out that I couldn't dress for the pleasures of others. That I had been doing it all wrong all along. That the clothes I decided to wear—or not wear—were solely up to me. My choice.

Until then, my clothing choices had been heavily dictated by Mom, my ex, the community. And I was done being told what to do. My modest way of dress started to change to shorter shirts and tighter jeans. With that came a sense of empowerment for me, but with that also came a brand-new kind of consumption by men.

11. SEX OBJECT

A week before my divorce was finalized, my friend suggested that we go to Miami for her birthday. I was apprehensive, but it was free lodging, so I couldn't beat that.

We went to this very cool club. There were really fine white dudes, Latinos, and Africans. Just a melting pot of fineness, unlike here in Detroit. Although I wasn't looking to find anyone, I just wanted to twerk freely in my newfound freedom. Shit on top of shit was piling up at home, and this was going to be my last vacation for a while.

I was dancing with my friends, hype as hell, and this guy kept bumping into me. The club was packed; whatever, I thought. He smoothly moved from behind to in front of me. He wanted some. We danced together for like two songs without saying a word to each other. He finally put his mouth to my ear. "What's your name?"

"Leah!" I shouted over the pulsating beats. "What's yours?"

"Marcus." He pulled back and smiled.

"Back That Azz Up" by Juvenile started playing. "This is my song!" he said and took my hand, leading me through the packed bodies and into the middle of the dance floor.

Not gonna even lie, that was my shit too.

He pulled me close, not in a creepy way. So I went with it.

My eyes were closed, and I was just savoring the moments, the company, and the music. I was in the zone.

"Leah?" My eyes popped back open, and I focused on him. "Look behind you."

I turned my head over my shoulder and saw some thinner girls standing around the bar sipping their drinks and staring at us tear up the dance floor.

"What?" I said, smiling.

"Make those skinny bitches mad."

He said it over and over again in my ear.

I melted like the ounce of sweet-cream butter I plop into the scolding hot pan when I make my fat-ass pancakes on Saturday mornings. Usually in the clubs, a scene like this would be reversed. All the thin girls would be the center of attention on the dance floor. They'd be the first ones to get chosen for a twerk/grind session while people like me were left to watch, only dreaming of being fifty pounds lighter to get the same amount of attention. It's sad. But it's true.

In Miami, the playing field had shifted. And I was soaking all of that shit in.

Until the age of twenty-nine, I'd only experienced one dick. My ex-hubby's. I know, so un-American. Throughout our ten-year relationship, I always wondered what other dick felt like, but I quickly pushed those thoughts away because I was going to be with him forever and ever and ever and ever.

After the divorce, I went to bookstores, lounges, meetups, house parties, and business events, looking to meet someone, but everyone was too scared to talk to one another. So, naturally, I gave up and gave in to the app life. Apps make people more comfortable. You can semi-screen a person before you actually meet up. But apps are as bad as real-life dating because unlike in person, you can manipulate images and bios easily. If you're fat, you can hit 'em with that angle and add lots of selfies. Got acne?

Don't worry about it, just smooth it a little here and here. Short as fuck? Hey, just have your friend kneel down, then take the pic so the camera adds a few more inches.

I had a few—well, many—failed dates, and I was over it after only two whole weeks.

Out of the blue, this Southern guy messaged me. I squinted my eyes and pursed my lips. "Who dis?" I asked my phone, as I glanced at the unread message.

He hadn't asked for nudes or my hip width. He was cute. Well traveled. And he could hold my attention for more than three minutes.

"Let's go to brunch," he insisted.

I clutched my imaginary pearls. I fuckin' loved brunch!

I tried to take the not-so-aggressive approach and asked him for recommendations. We ended up choosing one closest to an event I was cohosting that morning. I got semi-dressed up, making sure to wear my Spanx, just in case my stomach rolls scared him, and put on light makeup. He came up from behind me. We shared a friendly hug. He was a few inches taller than me. Score. He had brown hair, but his beard was on the reddish side. Half-ginger. Score! He had a bit of a Southern accent. I melted.

Now, there were downsides. He came in with what looked like basic-white-man-wear, aka I just kinda rolled out of bed and changed my shirt. Not gonna lie, it was freezing outside, and it was early Sunday morning. I let that slide. He didn't compliment me on my obvious casual chic look. I mean, it just would've added to his Southern charm. The waitress ended up complimenting me instead. "Oh my," she said, looking me up and down. "You are beautiful. Doesn't she look beautiful?" She looked at him.

He smiled. "She does."

Mind you, the restaurant was in a predominantly Black area. And he was white-white. You know how some white people who've lived in a bubble their whole lives get frazzled by being around too many people of color? He didn't do that. He told me that he was from Atlanta and lived in the ghettos and the 'burbs, so he had a good understanding of both worlds. Cultured and partially woke. Check. He told me about his trip to Spain, where he ran with the bulls. His travels to Europe and backpacking and hiking. He was an outdoorsman. Nice. I wasn't into being outside, but I could appreciate a man who was. He was an engineer at one of the Big-Three car companies. He had just moved to Royal Oak with his buddy. He didn't plan on living in Michigan for more than two years. He was funny and cool. I told him we could go to some shows downtown, since he was new and didn't know the spots. He said sure.

The checks were brought to the table. He didn't scramble to pay for my meal. But it was fine. Millennial dating, I guessed.

We walked to our cars, and I told him that I had a nice time and then I hit 'em with the "See ya round."

He stood by my car door. "Hey, what are you doing tonight?"

I thought about it. "Nothin' much."

"Well, since you like scary movies, we maybe could watch one at my place. That's if you're not busy."

I smiled. "How can I resist?"

"Then I'll text ya later then." He nodded.

"Cool."

My event was over, and I was dead tired. I went home and crashed, waking up hours later, around eight o'clock. There was a missed text from Southern Boy: "still on for tonight?"

I went to the gym, then looped back home and took a quick shower. He sent me the address, and I called my friend on the road.

"So, I met this guy and he's adorbs. Headed over there now to watch a movie," I gushed.

My friend repeated, "A movie?"

"Uh, yeah." She heard what I said the first time.

"Hmm, sounds like Netflix and chill."

I screamed. "What?"

"I'm just telling you what it sounds like. He didn't pay for your meal and now he wants you to watch a 'movie'? Why can't he take you to the theatre?"

"Well, obviously, it's a Sunday and he works in the AM." I pulled out whatever excuses I could find.

She sniffed. "Text me his address just in case you die."

"I love the reassurance you give me on the daily."

I was minutes away, and now I was feeling apprehensive. Maybe it was a ploy to get in my large undies. Maybe he was just like the rest of the fuck boys, and he was just better at hiding it. Maybe I should've texted him and be like, hey, not here to fuck, so if that's what you want, we can end this shit right here, right now.

But then I didn't want to sound crazy. I didn't want to be that person who assumed he only wanted to smash. What if I said all that, and he'd be like, that wasn't my intention. Then I'd look uber-stupid and he'd be weirded out, then never want to speak to me again.

I allowed my friend to get in my head. Now, I was unsure about it all. But I had already driven all the way and was parked in front of his condo. I sent my friend his picture, address, and phone number, then walked up to his door. I knocked. He answered. I stepped in, and he was drastically shorter than earlier. We were like face-to-face. I don't really have a thing for short dudes, so he lost about two more points.

"Nice place you have," I said.

"Yeah, it's me and my pal's place. He's out of town right now."

Oh, Lord. We were in the house. Alone.

He led me through the kitchen. "The TV room is in the basement."

"Oh," I replied.

"Want something to drink?"

"Nah, I got fucked up last night, so I'm gonna be sober until next Friday." My mind was still on the basement.

I allowed him to walk first, just in case I had to bust him over the side of the head and dip out. The room he led me to was completely furnished. It had a huge TV in the corner, video consoles underneath it, wires meandered every which way. Along the ceiling were vines of little colorful light bulbs. There was a glass table and couch. An American flag hung on the wall. Did he know I was Muslim? I knew he was from the South, but I hoped he didn't root for the Confederates.

I took a seat, as he fumbled with the remote. He turned on *Insidious*. Then plopped down beside me. We made stupid jokes and watched intently as things started to get spooky on the screen. I began to shiver really bad, despite having on a hoodie and thick socks.

"You okay?"

"No, actually I'm anemic. I get cold really easily. Do you have a blanket?"

"Yeah, sure." He paused the movie and reemerged with a comforter.

I burrowed myself in that blanket, and we continued to watch intently, making our little commentary on what we would've done if we were being chased by a weird creature. Unfortunately, twenty minutes passed, and I was still very cold.

"Warm enough?" he asked.

"This is gonna sound crazy, but do you have another blanket?"

He put the movie on pause again, then emerged with another comforter. He placed it over me, but this time he got underneath it. Our thighs touched as he leaned in closer. His body heat actually made me warmer.

Repeat: we were both under the blanket. Two blankets. Together. Alone in a big condo.

At one point, he threw his arm over my shoulder. I'm awkward. He probably expected me to maybe move closer and maybe lean in; instead I sat there like a board. He got the hint and took his arm away. His failed attempt at an advance hadn't fazed him though.

The movie came to an end, and he turned on *SpongeBob*. We chatted about the characters and our favorite episodes. He tried to sing one of the songs and fucked up the words. We laughed about that. It was getting late. He kept checking his watch, and his eyes were getting red. I knew he had to work in the AM and was probably tired.

"Well, this was fun. I should get going." I scooted to the edge of the couch to slip my shoes on, while he kind of lay back casually against the cushion. Now, everyone knows that I have a pretty huge bottom, and when I sit down, it spreads out even more, causing an illusion of layers and layers of ass, which causes some guys to fall into a tizzy.

As I struggled to get my foot inside the mouth of the shoe, he was silent. I looked back over my shoulder to catch him intensely staring at my butt. His eyes paused there for at least two seconds, then they slowly crawled up my back and then stopped at my face. He'd been a gentleman the entire time, I thought. He's allowed one look. One lingering look laced with objectifiable thoughts. I could handle that.

I sighed. Then put the other shoe on. Once again, I looked over my shoulder, and he was dead ass staring at my derriere with a look similar to that of a hyena that hadn't eaten in a long, long time. I stood up quickly. "Thanks for the movie."

We walked up the stairs, and I waited for him to go in front of me, but instead he motioned for me to go first. I gave a nervous chuckle and gulped. It seemed that the basement stairs had quadrupled. I'd have to walk about six flights as he basically had the pleasure of sticking his face in my ass and watching it bounce and jiggle with each step. If I ran, he'd get enjoyment. If I walked slowly and tightened my butt cheeks so they'd have minimal shake, he'd get enjoyment. There was no backing out and no way to walk. I was getting eye-raped.

I took the railing and walked at a normal pace as he walked behind me. I could feel his presence with each step, higher and higher. I waited for the inevitable ass smack so that I could turn around and smack the shit out of him.

I finally made it to the top. Relieved that he hadn't tried anything.

I was at the door. He said goodnight. We hugged. Then I walked to my car. I called my friend, almost in tears.

"He wanted to—to Netflix and chiiiiiiiiiiill."

She sucked her teeth. "Told ya."

"I'm so over dating. Men are gross."

"Sounds like a plan."

"Did you cook?"

"Yup."

"Is there enough for me?"

"Oh, my God."

"What? All that pent-up sexual tension from old boy got me hungry."

■　■　■　■

I stewed on how men could play the field and fling their dicks around, and no one batted an eyelash. I was sick and tired of playing the "good" Muslim role, while everyone else went ahead and lived their lives. I was in control. Like a man. And I had something to prove with my sexuality.

I downloaded the holy grail of fuckery: Tinder. Tinder was like meth. Ya just didn't dabble in it. Ever. Swiping left and right became an addiction. I had guys asking me to blow them, send nudes, or partake in threesomes. None of which were happening.

One white dude messaged me on Tinder. He wanted to come over for "cuddles." Sounded shady as fuck, but I'd been chatting with him for a week, so it wasn't too dangerous, I justified to myself. I mean, I knew if someone was a killer or not in a week.

On the way to my place, he got lost and told me that he was headed back home. White boy code for: I'm from the 'burbs, I'm scared, and I can't handle the pressure.

I'd already put clothes on, so I decided to just meet him at a coffee shop. He sat in his truck. I hopped in and gave him a hug to break the ice. He was little. I like my mens tall, but hey, beggars can't be choosers. He was very much so white. Like, I grew up in the suburbs of Ohio and then moved to the suburbs of Michigan white.

He had these sleepy blue eyes and sandy brown hair with a Bieber flip in the front. Although small, he was fit. We drove around in the chilly night and chatted. Then he pulled over and cut the lights.

"I work in landscaping," he said massaging his shoulder. "My neck and back are killing me."

"Oh," I said thoughtfully. "You're in luck because I'm pretty good at massages." Direct hit.

Sandy's sleepy eyes lit. "Right now?"

He turned his back toward me. I placed my hands on his shoulders and worked my magic. Firm, you could tell he worked out. After a few minutes, my arms got tired. I patted his shoulders. "All done."

He flicked his Bieber bang. "I wish you'd never stop." Then his hand creeped on my knee.

"I've got to pee," I blurted. Ship sinking. Abort. Abort!

"Oh, okay." He removed his hand, then started the engine.

When I got home, I was sexually frustrated and mad that I hadn't just come out and said it: I'm going through a divorce, I need to flex my muscle, and I'd like to sleep with your little white ass. Who was I turning into? Meeting dudes off the internet? Seeing them late at night? I wasn't a tenderoni anymore.

It didn't stop there.

I masked empowerment with recklessness and found myself sending dirty snaps to guys at 1 a.m., fuck-boy time, and partaking in sexting, trying to find the right angles to show my ass in a pair of skimpy undies. Just to feel something. I'd become the girl that I never wanted to be. Crazed, impulsive, and obsessive would be a few choice words I'd use to describe myself freshly post-divorce. I thought that if I could get attention from these men, my grief would, poof, disappear. That if I slathered icing on shit, it'd kill the smell.

The funny thing was that at the time, I was still blogging about intersectional feminism and objectification, when behind closed doors, I was blatantly objectifying myself. Such a fraud, I thought. But none of that mattered, because in my head, once I upped my body count, I'd be fulfilled and turn the tables on the male race that thought only they could be the players of the world.

I was going to put out to the first dude that offered.

In the following weeks, another opportunity arose. I started talking to Tats because he had a ton of tattoos and I can't remember his name. We talked back and forth for about two weeks. We decided to meet up after my friend's birthday party.

The house was full of drinks and people. My friends and I danced. Drank. Laughed. Roasted one another. It was a good time. I got a text from Tats asking if we were still on. He wanted to come over after work. My eyes sparkled. There was a possibility that I'd finally add a body to my count.

My friend wanted to sleep over that night. I told her, "Possible dick appointment. I'll let ya know."

She high-fived me.

We got ridiculously wasted. I mean, we were all done. We ended up going to the club. Fists pumping. Hair flicking. Twerking. Weird Indian dudes. It was a blur. One by one, we all left the club, agreeing it was an epic evening/morning.

At home, I struggled to get up the stairs. On all fours like a dog, climbing the steps to my lady cove. I needed to clean before Tats arrived. There were clothes and accessories everywhere. Makeup was strewn about on my dresser. Blankets on the floor. I plopped down on the couch and almost passed out. I made it back downstairs to wash the sweat of the club from my body. I peeled my shirt off. Then the pants. I sloppily washed my cooch. And dragged myself back up the stairs.

For a moment, I asked: Are you really going to be this sleazy? Are you really going to fuck a stranger you don't know and never met before in person?

Yes.

I heard a knock at the door.

I'm kind of night blind, so a Caucasian arm reached out and grabbed my hand. It was very mysterious and sexy. I handed him a towel, and he took a shower downstairs as my roommate slept. I told him I'd be upstairs, waiting.

Although I was exhausted from partying, I lay there in my bed with the haze of the TV playing *Bob's Burgers*. I heard the water from the shower head turn off. Some rustling. Then the door to my attic bedroom opened and closed. Footsteps. I was under a blanket in full clothes. He only had a towel on. I saw all of his colorful tattoos and his dark hair and blue eyes. It was really happening. I thought maybe we'd chat first. Nope. He slipped into my bed like he knew me or something. He grabbed me and kissed me with his thin, cold lips. A complete stranger. It was fascinating and immoral simultaneously.

"Sorry." I pulled back. "I smell like weed and liquor."

He smiled. "It's okay."

Although I can't remember his name, I remember he was rough. At one point, he thought my cooch was a slice of chocolate cake and dove in.

I screeched. Which meant, my shit was a delicate flower, bro!

Afterward, I lay there nude, with the blanket covering half my body, as he immediately got up and got dressed. He made small talk. I was uninterested. I hadn't felt anything. It was as if nothing happened at all. I told him that I'd lock the door behind him. My main concern was that he didn't steal any of my roommate's shit on the way out.

I passed out shortly after.

The next morning, I was sore and partially hung over. I sat on my bed and read my missed text messages. It was him. Tats. *Oh God.* I thought these things were like a hit, quit, and forget. You didn't chat like old friends afterward. He said: your ass is amazing. I didn't answer for hours because I didn't know what to say. So, the next day, I texted him back: thanks.

He hadn't said that my mind was amazing or that he enjoyed our conversation. He'd fixated on a part of my body. The part that always seemed to be objectified, not only by white men but every man, Muslim dudes included.

As I found myself reducing him to a body part to prove a point of post-divorce sexual prowess, the idea that I could be "bad" too, that I could break the rules, he had in return reduced me to a body part.

I'd become the fat girl who is an easy lay because she desperately needed to be touched. The one chubby chasers only give physical attention to in the dark. The girl who straight-sized men tried out because they'd "never been with a fat girl before."

I know that all women go through insecurities on some level, but since fatphobia is so ingrained in our society, it's hard not to think that people will sleep with you in private, but never show you off to their friends or family, because of the embarrassment of your fatness. They are conditioned to see fat people as funny friends, sidekicks to attractive thin folk, or an easy fuck, because clearly fat people are just happy to get any kind of attention.

We aren't the main leads in action films, the sexy heroines in form-fitting bodysuits, the stand-alone characters in erotica novels. We are the backgrounds.

This very toxic ideology lingers above me each and every time I try to enter into a relationship, every time I think a cute guy likes me. When I believe that I am undeserving based solely on how I look. And I hate it so much. The question is, Do they not like me or aren't attracted to me because I am big?

On the last day of my *Eat Pray Love* London trip, I was pick-pocketed in a muggy club in Brixton called Dogstar. Although angered, I wasn't going to let that fuck up my London experience.

As I entered Dogstar, the moisture from the overly packed club fogged my artsy shades. I made my way across the wet and sticky dance floor full of crunched cups and spilled beer to the coat check.

Although the club was diverse, there were a lot of Europeans. As I pushed through tight-packed bodies and got a whiff of all the different odors, ranging from musty to fresh but mostly funky, I hit the dance floor. Just hoping that they didn't play a bunch of bad music. Shit that I couldn't bounce to. Because bad music was the way to make any Black girl abandon that bitch with the quickness.

I'm the kind of clubber that has no chill. They played a Bey song, and I took my dancing to a level ten. Full on moves. When Beyoncé played in the club, you had to pay homage. It was only right. So, I was doing my thing, oblivious to everyone else, and I felt a tap on my shoulder. I looked over, and it was a Middle Eastern–looking dude. Cute face, hair laid but short. I scrunched my nose, internally. Not into shorties. Two shorts didn't make a right in my book. He gave me a huge smile, then shot me a thumbs-up. Cute. I smiled back. Maybe he was just being nice.

Again, he tapped my shoulder and held his hand in the air for a high five. I hit it and thought that was pretty whimsical. He smiled that huge, welcoming smile. Again, I turned around and started dancing, alone.

Next moment, a trap song played. I got super hype. I was in London!

And there he was back for the third time, standing right next to me. He played it cool, bobbing his head, trying so hard to be incognito. I rolled my eyes and shimmied a bit. He tapped my arm. I looked over. He placed one finger up, then began to type on his smartphone. After he finished the sentence, he handed me the phone: "Are you alone?"

Instantly, I knew he was a creep. "What kind of question is that?" I yelled over the music.

He waved his hand in protest, then typed: "I mean, are you single?"

"Oh," I said. "Yup."

His fingers moved wildly over the letters: "I like the way you dance."

"Oh, thanks."

I took his phone and typed: "Why do you keep typing?"

Taking the phone back, he replied: "I'm deaf."

My eyes widened. "Ohhhhhhh."

This entire time, he'd been trying to flirt using nonverbal cues that I'd been totally dismissing.

I asked him, "Do you want to dance?"

He watched my lips move intently, then he nodded vigorously. I put my arms around his neck and shoulders, and he placed his hands on my waist, and we danced for a song. Afterward, one of his friends came up, and he had to go. But before he left, I told him that I was going to head out as well. He placed one finger up, wanting me to wait.

"Fine," I said. "Then, I'm going home."

Five minutes later he resurfaced and motioned for me to follow him outside.

"Going home," I reminded him.

He looked at my mouth. "I go," he mouthed. He pulled out his phone and typed: "I'll walk you home."

"That's very nice of you." I was lost anyway, so having a guide at three o'clock in the morning was handy. "But what about your friends?"

He typed: "They are fine."

We walked to the bus stop in the cold Brixton streets where white partygoers stumbled from bars and women in six-inch heels and furry coats chased down buses. He pulled out a bag of Arabic tobacco and rolled it into a cigarette.

"Are you from the Middle East?"

He typed with a lit cig in the corner of his mouth: "Mom from South Africa. Dad from Pakistan."

"Cool mix."

"Yeah, yeah," he mouthed, smiling. I wondered if he was really that happy or if the huge smiles were a mechanism he used to compensate for his inability to speak. All in all, I was completely fascinated with him.

It was probably stupid looking back on it, but I asked, "Do you sign?"

"Yeah." He nodded.

He put my address into the GPS, and we waited for bus 118 to Stratham Commons in a crowd full of people in front of a Kentucky Fried Chicken spot.

I was freezing after sweating in the club, and the cold air was seeping into my open pores. Shivering, I pulled my coat closed as my teeth chattered. He took my arm and pulled me in, then held me close. People were around. PDA was frowned upon in the US. PDA with a fat girl was even more frowned upon. My body stiffened as I kept trying to make small talk to lessen my awkwardness in his arms. That question, that same question, arose like a mighty sword. Is he uncomfortable with my body? He is little and I am big.

I thought about dumb things like, was his arm able to reach all the way around my body, that if I was smaller in circumference his arm would definitely be able to fit all the way around. Then and only then, I could be dainty and fragile and cute. How big had I looked in comparison to him? Had we looked odd together in the eyes of the people surrounding us because he was slim and I was fat? Was he doing this because he felt pity for me or because he genuinely really liked a strange Black girl from the club?

I looked into his face, you know, since I was so close, to try and figure out his motives. The only one I was met with was the warmth of his hazel-green eyes.

His hair was faded perfectly, not one hair out of place, with gentle waves at the top. The softness of his beard grazed my cheek, and the scent was fresh yet manly.

He had a sweetness about him that made me feel less awkward, less body conscious, and warm, less like the usual tense me. The shields I had up, the questions that were swirling about my fatness, dissolved. What the hell was happening?

The only thing I was able to get out was, "You have pretty eyes."

He smiled. His usual response.

The bus came, and we swiped our Oyster cards. He led me to the second level and all the way to the back. I guessed cuz we had a long ride ahead of us, but I hadn't felt the need to question anything else. There were crumbs on the seat. He wiped them away hastily and motioned for me to sit when it was clean. He placed his arm around me, and I leaned in without the clumsiness of before. He took my hand and intertwined his fingers through mine and squeezed. I peeked at him and giggled, not knowing what else to do. This was all so foreign to me. My eyes darted from head to head, as I wondered what people thought of our affection.

As I looked ahead, I felt him looking at me, burning the side of my face with his gaze. In my peripheral, I noticed him staring at my lips. But I wasn't talking, so I believed that he wanted a taste. I wasn't comfortable though. I'd glance at him every once in a while to see if he'd changed his mind, but he just continued staring.

He kissed my cheek. It was sweet.

I turned to him and kissed his lips. I wondered if my breath smelled. When I pulled back, he caressed my cheek and kissed me again, on the lips, that time much longer. He tasted of faint tobacco and coconuts. I bit his bottom lip, then pulled back, nestling my head in his shoulder. I looked around the bus once more at the back of people's heads and waited for that one person to turn around and scream, "Get a room." But everyone was stashed away in their own little universes.

And we were in ours.

That was a such a defining moment for me. That size hadn't been a factor. That there are people in the world that truly accept me for me, as a human being.

12. PERFECTLY IMPERFECT

"What's your obsession with being perfect?" The therapist sat across from me in a small, yet comfy therapy room.

I looked down at my hands that lay flat on my big thighs. "It's all I know how to be."

She nodded. "How long has this obsession been going on?"

"Ever since I can remember," I replied. "Overachieving, being better than someone else makes me feel good."

"Was your father or mother an overachiever?"

"I don't know much about my dad," I sniffed. "Maybe, my mom. But she was just, very confident. You know, kind of cocky almost. She just had high standards for herself and others."

"By others, you mean you and your siblings?"

I nodded. "Everyone."

"Did she ever belittle you, growing up?"

My shoulders got tense. "Yeah, but it was just small stuff."

"Hmm, what kind of small stuff?"

"Well, one time, she had lost a lot of weight and I was still pretty chubby. She was in the basement exercising, and I had come down to ask her something. Can't remember what exactly, and she made a snarky comment about my body."

"Which was?"

"She said, 'You're just mad because you're jealous of how my body looks.'"

"How'd that make you feel?"

"I was shocked that she was making me feel bad about being fat. She was my mom. I thought moms were supposed to make you feel good, confident."

"Interesting."

"I don't know. Growing up, I just felt like nothing I ever did was right. I needed validation, and the only way I could get it was by being perfect. Doing more than the next person. It gave me control. Something I lacked when I was growing up. Control brings stability for me. And stability is safe. Perfection is key. If I can be perfect, then I'd never have any problems."

"Are you ready for a minor dose of reality?" Her eyes narrowed.

"Shoot."

"Name a perfect person who's thin, has gorgeous skin, has all the money in the world, and never, ever makes mistakes."

I thought about it. No name came up.

"I'll give you another minute." She sat back.

"I can't name one."

She smirked. "Are you some kind of extraterrestrial being that I don't know of?"

I shook my head.

"So, let me get this straight. You are a human just like me and just like your mother. But in your mind, you believe that you can be a perfect entity in this world. Yet, you can't even name a perfect person. Not one. Perfection isn't real, Leah. Never was and never will be. Why strive for something that's not attainable and torture yourself in the process like you've been doing. And by no means am I saying to not set or achieve goals, but I can only imagine the stress you put yourself through trying to grab something that you'll never be able to touch."

My therapist was like Dr. Phil. She always gave me the simplest, most commonsense advice, but each and every time, it blew my fuckin' mind. I had never learned that perfection wasn't real growing up. Perfection existed all around me, or so I believed, and I policed myself to attain it.

But she was right. I *was* torturing myself trying to be the smartest, the thinnest, the most well-spoken Black girl on the block. Why couldn't I just be content with trying my best? And wherever I landed was where I was actually meant to be?

To accept that fact was okay.

I wasn't missing out on the first-place crown at the Perfection Pageant.

What I was gaining, instead, was an identity. A true one. And I was taking the steps to becoming perfectly imperfect. Which was the me I've always wanted to be all along.

■　■　■　■

You'd be cuter if you lost weight. No one is gonna want you that big. Are you too thick? Here's a diet plan. You are too big to model. Big girls are easy. They'll put out and settle for anything. Are you pregnant? You look like the Charmin Bear. I'm tired of seeing fat people. Fat people are always wearing bright colors; why would they want to add any extra attention to themselves? I Googled "fat, ugly Muslim" and you popped up. You are a bad role model for kids. You are glorifying obesity. You'll end up dying at forty-five.

These are only a handful of troll-ish comments that I've received.

I don't think that thinner people can ever fathom the fat-person narrative, the struggle of everyday life. And no, I'm not asking for sympathy, because some of us are fat by choice, but there are countless others who genetically were never meant to be small and/or have a very hard time losing and maintaining a "socially acceptable" weight.

"Your aunt can't get a job because she's fat," Mom had said matter-of-factly to my younger sister and me. I was thirteen. And I remember thinking, *That's not the reason why. It's just a bad economy.*

Although Mom wasn't as big as my aunt, her weight was up and down. Mostly up. She had suffered from eating disorders for most of her life. To be honest, I never really recalled Mom eating "real food" like the stuff she fed us. She was a closet eater who binged on cakes and doughnuts in the privacy of her bedroom. The sheets would be riddled with crumbs, the aroma of sugary frosting lingering in the air.

Mom showed us old photos of her younger, thinner self in the '70s with her short shorts and crop top on, rocking a thick, black Afro. She said proudly, while pointing, "See? My thighs didn't touch back then. When they touched, I knew that I was eating too much." Thin was good in our house. Great even. Fat was unacceptable.

And I was fat.

My thighs touched. My belly hung over my panties. My boobs jumped when I jumped. My double chin greeted you before I was able to. My arms squeezed into jackets that didn't stretch.

When I sat down, I used to sit up straight and suck my stomach in. I'd order only water, maybe a Diet Pepsi. Lie and tell my thin friends at the table that I had already eaten at home, that I was full. A few would roll their eyes; others would hunch their shoulders and begin ordering everything off the menu. Every fatty thing that had made me the way I currently was. Very fat. Morbidly obese, as the doc would say, with a click of the tongue and slow shake of the head. I hated going to the doctor, by the way. You only got praised when the number on the scale went down from the previous visit—didn't matter if you had gout or measles.

Do you have any idea what it was like to be fat in the early 2000s, when I was just hitting puberty? Britney and Christina and Alicia Silverstone and Gwen Stefani were hella popular. White girls with bleach-blonde hair, hip bones that peeked over their low-ride jeans, crop tops, tube tops, and frayed shorts, and little perky boobs. Straight teeth and pouty lips with layer upon layer of gloss that smelled like strawberries. It was no better in the African American community. Although they were a little thicker, artists like Alicia Keys, Beyoncé, and Lil' Kim still had flat tummies and fit arms.

The only fat people I had to look up to were Louie Anderson, Roseanne Barr, and Mimi from *Drew Carey*. They weren't fashionable by any means nor were they ever seen as bombshells, but they were fuckin' hilarious.

So, that's what I was going up against, and I lost right off the bat. Society didn't tell me that I was worthy or cute. It told me that I would always be friend-zoned, that if a guy liked me, it was because he was under the assumption that I was easy, since, ya know, my self-esteem just had to be below zero, and if he was to have a relationship with me, then it'd have to be on the down-low because he wouldn't want to have his friends and family find out that he was a chubby chaser. Liking a big girl was like some sort of illness. I mean, who in their right mind would find someone with a bit more blubber attractive, lovable? Unheard of!

I was mesmerized by these images and ideas. And I believed skinny was better. Attainable.

That's when my life took a turn. I remember picking up a pair of stylish jeans that were three sizes too small. They were going to be my staple. The mark that would validate me in my quest for perfection. In my head, I was going to die to get into those jeans if necessary. I hung them up so I could see them when I first woke up, when I studied, or laid my head down to sleep. I wanted them to be a reminder of what I could be if I could just pull them over my legs and zip them comfortably.

Instead of motivating me to eat healthier, the jeans taunted me. They became the crux of failure every time I'd pull them off the hanger and unsuccessfully tug them up my wide-set hips. With every yank of the material, I'd sink lower and lower into the sunken place.

Self-worth was a roller coaster, and mine was usually attached to what I could and couldn't fit into. I developed an eating disorder and as a result once lost seventy pounds. And how things changed. Everyone was sooooo happy. It was as if I had won some sick lottery. My teachers, everyone from teens to adults, asked me how I'd done it.

"It's easy," I lied.

Guys started to notice me. Girls were jealous of me.

At home, when the cheers died, and I was all alone, I was still fat. Inside. The scale said one thing, but my mind told me another.

Losing the weight was brutal. Maintaining it was different. My antics got wilder, as I scrambled to stay thin. In the morning, I'd clear my bowels and bladder, strip butt-ass naked, and get on the scale. If the scale was even a pound heavier, my entire day would be ruined. If the scale was in the negative, the day would be amazing, because I was closer to being skinnier. I was on the no-carb diet, so I peed on a stick twice a day (sometimes three) to see if I was in optimal ketosis—fat-burning mode. I'd frequently chew on no-sugar sticks of gum to curb my appetite. I'd go through packs and packs of gum. Mom bought them in bulk from Costco. She was trying to lose weight too. I'd strip again in the evening and slide on the scale. Then I'd turn on the Style Network and watch models strut down the runway in expensive clothes, and I'd cry.

Nothing ever lasted.

I gained back all the weight, plus another fifty pounds.

After that, there were years that I wouldn't step on a scale. I'd arch my back and hiss at the sight of one. It became the omen. Even when I got my mandatory checkups, I'd close my eyes or step on the scale backward (Aha! Didn't know that trick did ya?). I basically wrote the fat girl's guide to ignoring your weight.

Any weight with 2- on it is bad, but when you had a 3- in front of your weight, OMG, why the fuck aren't you dead yet?

Although I dodged the scale, there were some things an obese girl like myself couldn't ignore. And I've noticed that many people who have body issues do a helluva lot of online shopping, because of the dreaded fitting room. That room is unforgiving. The too-bright lighting, the three-way mirrors, and the clothes. The garments only go up to a certain size. And of course, I grabbed the biggest ones. If I went past the largest size they had, I'd be falling into the rack and stumbling upon Ashley Stewart Narnia, and that'd be a whole other issue.

I'd feel hopeful if I could comfortably fit into three out of the ten items I'd grabbed. And if one or two items out of those choices hid my under-belly roll, then it was going to be a good fuckin' day.

Regular bathroom lighting does a fat nude body like mine justice. The fitting room mirror gave zero fucks about my feelings. Before I even had a chance to try on the first probably-too-squishy shirt, I stared at my arms. The women in my family had big-ass arms. Thanks, Mom! I lifted my arms out to the side and watched those large flaps of extra skin dangle from the actual bicep. Then I wiggled them like bat wings and watched as they go, go, go. *Why the fuck are my arms so big?* Then I zoomed into my breasts. They looked like I've had eleven kids and counting. They were flat like pancakes, like an orangutan, all elasticity somehow sucked out, and to top it off, one was bigger than the other. I held them up to see what they'd look like if I had a Kardashian chest. I let them go, and they both flopped back to position. In a very un-Kardashian fashion. *Fuck me.* Oh, the stomach. It was like a vertical rolling hill. It just seemed to roll and roll like a snowman's, getting bigger and bigger until you got to the bottom where the massive fat roll resided.

"'Sup?" Fat Roll said to me.

I lifted my chin in acknowledgment. "So, you shoppin'?"

"Stop talking to me." I gave it the evil eye.

It shrugged. "So touchy."

I grabbed it from the bottom and lifted the slab attached to my body and held the thirty pounder in my hands. Stretch marks lined it like it'd been clawed by a big cat. Then I did the "jiggle dance." I squeezed it and mashed it and jumped up and down. Just hoping that despite my eating habits, it'd just fall right off onto the dusty floor and I could quickly grab my things and run before it noticed I was gone. And the last thing I abused was my thighs. They were 90 percent cellulite. On top of that, I had these huge fat pockets on the sides. Again, like I was carrying triplets. One dude told me once that I had good child-bearing hips. I shuddered and disappeared into the darkness.

After all of that was done, it was time to try on the clothes.

I pulled the shirt over my head, which emerged like a newborn crowning. So far, so good. Then I pulled my arms through the narrow slits they called sleeves. It got tighter and tighter as my arms moved through. Then I pulled the rest of the fabric down the rolling-hill belly. The three-way mirror sniggered. Was I in a clothing store located in Asia or was I in America? I looked like David Banner bursting out of his work shirt, transitioning into the Hulk.

The pants. They looked big as hell on the hanger, so they must fit. Right? Wrong. One foot in. Pulled up to mid-thigh, and second foot in, pulled it up to mid-thigh. The moment of truth. The waist, which was very much so stretched to capacity, wouldn't ride smoothly over my kangaroo hip pockets. I jumped up and squeezed my butt cheeks together to allow at least two more inches to decrease. I popped my pelvis forward and shimmied. The pants said, "Not today, bitch."

I wished I had a glass of wine, so I could dramatically throw it at the mirrors, and they'd smash into a trillion pieces. But I knew the skinny white retail worker would call the 4–0 and I'd promptly be taken to jail and given a life sentence. I was Black and Muslim. I had to stay on the straight and narrow.

Then the internet was invented. Social media, to be exact, and it gave attention to underserved and underrepresented groups of people shunned by regular media outlets, redefining beauty and how "normal" folk internalized it and, of course, gave trolls another channel to hate and discriminate.

When my friends forced me to get an Instagram account, I was so over it. It was mainly to catch up on the Instagram beefs going down in the Muslim community, which were quite entertaining. Then I learned about the hashtag function. I put in

#plussizemodels, and an entire world opened. I had always been mistaken for a plus-size model, but I was never going to make it anywhere doing it as a career. Ha!

I started following Everything Curvy and Chic, Alysse Dalessandro, and Tess Holliday, and a slew of other models who also attached themselves to the "Body-Positive" movement. I couldn't believe my eyes. These girls had the biggest boobs, short bodies, large arms, and fat stomachs, and beat faces, bomb clothes, and professional photographers. They traveled the world. They started movements. They were feminist and making money. I mean, I'm sure they had issues, but as far as I could tell, they were living the life that I wanted to live. The life I had stopped myself from living because of the 2- and 3- before the number on the scale.

That kind of life with restrictions was tiring. And it was all my fault. I had allowed other people's comments about me being fat to hinder me from being Leah V. I allowed the media to tell me that the size-two white girl on the cover of *Vogue* set the only standards for beauty. I allowed myself to eat a handful of pretzels and gum just to stuff myself into a shape that I was never going to be able to maintain in the long run, and I had been doing it for so long that it became some normalized, fucked-up habit.

The day I stopped giving a fuck about the numbers on the scale and only about how I felt, was the day I was freed.

Once my brother-in-law got in my face and said in front of everyone, "You ain't nothin' but a fat bitch."

I got closer, using the two extra inches I had on him, and looked him dead in the eye, "Tell me something I don't know. Although, me being a bitch widely depends on who you ask."

He didn't even know what to say back.

That's what happened when you reclaimed shit! Words no longer crushed you into a million pieces.

Now, I'm mostly clean of eating disorders. I don't look at food the same way. Do I have my days where it's like, You really didn't need four scoops of ice cream? Sure, but do I allow it to define my self-worth? Definitely not. I'm far past that.

Unfortunately, my newfound fat freedom has caused quite a stir and has made other people uncomfortable, angry even. But when I was a sad fatty, no one had an issue with me hating myself and having an unhealthy mentality about my body. All was well with the world. But as soon as I started to become a confident fatty, then the trolls started to crawl from their lairs. *You're promoting obesity. Diabetes. And unhealthy living.* Ohhhh, am I? Last time I checked, I go to the gym at least five days a week, don't have diabetes or any other so-called "fat-related" ailments. I probably eat healthier than I ever have in my life. But the thing is, I don't have to explain that to you or anyone else. If someone chooses a lifestyle, then by all means, shoot for the stars. Whatever lifestyle that is.

"They're insecure and angry because they see you unapologetically fat. And although they don't struggle with a weight issue, they struggle with self-esteem," my friend told me.

Bingo!

Even though I'm a body-positive activist and comfortable with my body, there are times when I'm reminded of how disgusting other human beings can be toward fat people. And don't for one second think that fat people don't fat-shame other fat people. Oh, the irony!

The most forms of fat-shaming I've ever experienced have come on airplane rides. I squeeze through the narrow aisle, usually sideways because my hips and butt would smack every passenger's shoulder dangling over the sides of the armrests. No matter what angle I try, someone is getting bumped. I get nasty stares as they look my fat ass up and down. I try to keep my gaze lowered, but it's hard to see the seat assignments that way. Forced to make eye contact with people who are clearly disturbed by my hugeness, I breathe a sigh of relief when I find my seat.

One time, there were two people already occupying the seats. A thin, older white woman and a male. I was smack dab in the middle. The woman glared at me as if I was infringing upon her rights. I squished all my rolls past the one empty seat and plopped down in the middle. Now, everyone knows that coach seats aren't roomy. If you have long legs, you'll be cramped. If you have a big tummy, cramped. If all the seats are occupied, craaaaaaamped. It's just the name of the game.

As a very hippy woman, my thighs always get pinched between the seat arms. I can't even sit in lawn chairs because they pinch my damn legs. So, imagine a four-hour flight. Most of the time, the person beside me will notice that I'm in pain and lift the arm up, so that my hips can breathe. Which I'm so grateful for because they technically don't have to. I know my thigh meat is spilling into your seat and I'm sorry. This time, Miss Thin White Thang, slammed her armrest down. Nose pointed up. She wasn't giving me any leeway.

I'd usually place my coat over my lap and try to put my seatbelt on inconspicuously. Of course, that bitch was lacking about a foot of belt-strap length. I was too embarrassed to ask for an extender. For the entire flight, I just didn't wear a seatbelt at all. I've flown a few other times without wearing one. Looking back on it, I made the decision to risk my safety in order not to be embarrassed. I was willing to place my fat life on the line because of some thin bitch's judgmental eyes.

Another time, the two fattest passengers on the plane were seated next to each other, me and a really big white man. My hips were huge, and his shoulders were expansive. He had the window seat, and I had the middle. Between the both of us, we needed like legit three seats. We got a little close and personal. My fat was on him, and his fat was on me. I was okay with it, but he wasn't. He was huffing and puffing. I wanted to say, "Uhh, sir. You're fat as fuck like me. Get the fuck over it." Instead, I had no chill, fell asleep, and used his comfy shoulder as a pillow.

Now, when I fly, I push the call button and request a seatbelt extender, or I ask for it before I get to my seat. I have no shame in my game. I'm big, and I want to live in the event that the whole plane goes down and we crash on a deserted island. I just hope that the seatbelt can live up to its safety standards and hold my ass in place.

People who have body image issues always ask, "When did you become this?" And by "this," they mean this ball of not-giving-a-fuckery. I always say that it didn't happen all at once, but the turning point was when I got tired of using my fatness as an excuse not to live. I can't do that. I can't wear this. I can't date that person because how would they feel about being with a fat girl. My friends must be ashamed of me. When I eat, I know for a fact that people are watching, disgusted. That job I can never attain because my weight dictates my esteem level.

Staaawwwwwp!

We are all working with the body we have now, not the body we used to have or could have. It's great. Have body and health goals. I'm not advocating that you don't.

I've let it go. My goal is to be healthy. Happy. And free. Yes, I have my days where I believe that I'm a fat shit that no one will love or cherish. But the next day, I'll throw on a faux fur coat and waltz into the grocery store feeling like a million fat-ass bucks and can't nobody tell me shit.

But most of all, I think about all the time I wasted worrying about how not to be fat. How to take up as little space as possible. I wish that I could take my thirteen-year-old self's hand and show her a photo of herself now. Show her how curvy and jiggly and fabulous she looks. How she slays like a fat Amber Rose (since I've buzzed off all of my hair and dyed it platinum blonde). Tell her that the size she tried to attain would never make her truly happy. That it's perfectly fine to be imperfect and own every ounce of it. That she should take those jeans that were three sizes too small, go outside, light a fire, and toss them straight into the flame.

PART 5
UNAPOLOGETICALLY ME

. . . .

13. TO WEAR OR NOT TO WEAR

In Boston, my Somali friend and I scarfed down fried pickles and crab legs and chatted about good food, Islam, and being a woman in America.

"Ohh, let me see the photos from your trip to London," she exclaimed.

I swiped over to the photos that I took for this independent Muslim designer, Buno Design, that made these bomb handmade kimonos. The photographer was a Parisian hijabi. Even though I was tired from flying overseas, I had had approximately thirty minutes to rush to the shoot. I was totally surprised that the photos had come out so well.

The waitress came up behind my friend, who was admiring the photos.

"That's you?" The white female server asked, eyeing me with suspicion like she was a cop and I was a Black kid innocently walking on the sidewalk.

"It is." I lifted my chin.

"You a model?"

I raised a brow. "Yes."

"May I?" the waitress said, but more like demanded with her white privilege.

My friend handed her my phone. The white girl swiped right, seemingly puzzled. Every once in a while, she'd glance at me, then back at the photos. I waited for her to say something off the wall.

She finally handed the phone back. "Where were those taken?"

"London," I said modestly. "I had a few gigs there."

"You model with that on?" she pointed to my hijab. "All the time?"

"Yeah, I model with my hijab on."

Becky the waitress crossed her arms over her chest, trying to figure out how someone like me could model, how someone my size and in my religion could be living that kind of life that she had been told was only for thin, white women. She couldn't figure out how to compare me to the Muslims she'd seen on CNN or Fox News. The ones who were very Middle Eastern or very extreme.

"Where are you guys from?" she asked, continuing her interrogation tactics with the same stereotypical question that most Americans ask folks with hijabs. Because you just couldn't be totally American and wear hijab. You are automatically "other."

"I'm African American Muslim," I said with a smile.

My friend replied, "I'm Somali Muslim."

"Oh," Becky nodded. Then after an awkward pause, she said, "Those photos are really nice."

I yearned to reply "I know," but I said "Thanks" instead.

I knew she wanted to pry more into our lives but had other tables to wait. Or maybe she got the very real feeling that her delivery was all wrong and that her presence was annoying. Whichever one, she'd just been taught a lesson about stereotyping.

I've learned that the strong dislike of my choice of hijab is a personal and ignorant one.

After 9/11, many Americans bunched Muslims, usually the Black and brown ones, into one category. They accused us all of being extremists. We all carried weapons under our hijabs and were to be watched and patted down, taking extra precautions to maintain the safety of everyone else. We were soulless, barbaric, unable to empathize with anyone who wasn't Muslim. We were dehumanized by the media. Ostracized by neighbors and friends to the point where a lot of us were in fear of our lives and the safety of our communities. Many removed scarves and never let on that we were Muslim. We hid our faith in a land that was supposed to be free.

I remember one day when I was little, Mom took me to get my hair braided and beaded. OMG. I was sooooo ecstatic, and it was a change from my usual two cornrows. The beads were small and multicolored. When I walked or shook my head, they clinked together. I was fancy. I couldn't wait to show the kids in the neighborhood my new do.

Then Mom paid the stylist and handed me my scarf.

My eyes widened. I had to put that, the hijab, over my hair? I had to cover up the multicolored beads? No one would see it. I slowly took the scarf from her and tied it around my hair. My shoulders slumped, as I followed her to the minivan.

A braid lined with beads slipped out over my forehead. I played with it for a while, but feared that the beads would unravel, so I just tucked it back into my hijab.

In that moment, I didn't want to wear it anymore, but then I didn't have a choice. I was young, and I already knew Mom wouldn't allow it. I remember when I had major issues with the hijab. It made me stand out, made me different. And different wasn't in.

For the most part, I wore it because if I didn't, I thought it'd make Mom angry, disappointed in me somehow. But I didn't like the way it made me feel. It was a piece of long, draping cloth on my head that wasn't supposed to be serious, but *was*. People made such a big deal out of not seeing my hair that I started to view hijab as the problem and not society and how they viewed differences of other cultures and religions. I was too young to understand. So I blamed the hijab.

The hijab was also so closely connected to being a Muslim woman. A lot of us Muslims—sadly including myself at one point—looked down upon girls, women, who didn't opt to wear it. We called them weak. Ostracized them. Questioned their faith and asked what was so hard about wearing it. Didn't they love Allah enough? We had been conditioned to predict whether or not you were a "good" Muslim based on a piece of cloth.

I fell into that trap, that mentality, until I was faced with the same challenge: to wear or not to wear. My struggle with the hijab was more outward than I initially thought. When I was nineteen, my non-Muslim aunt said to me, "Out of all the kids, I thought you'd be the one to stop wearing your scarf." It hurt my damn feelings.

Even though I'd never taken it off in front of her, she sensed my indecision. For me, the hijab became safe, a habit. I wore it out of loyalty and not want. I snatched it off at night when I was going out to party. I just wanted to be without the attachments of it, but its presence would always resurface.

I'd show my ID to the bouncer, and he'd stare at it for a long time, then glance up at me. My ID showed a hijabi. The girl who stood in front of him was a regular girl just wanting to have a good time. One bouncer was so brazen as to ask where my hijab was. I snatched my ID from him and stormed into the club.

How dare he? I thought. Then the following question was, *Why wasn't my hijab on my head?*

■ ■ ■ ■

The identity battle with my hijab continued well into adulthood. As I started to come to terms with it, that it was in fact my choice to wear it or not, others' disdain for it mounted.

I was hyperaware of my surroundings when I wore it, especially around white folks—they were the ones doing the most when it came to assaults and verbal attacks. I was lucky that I didn't live in the South where bigots gave zero fucks about putting their hands on you if they thought in their little minds that you were Muslim. Although I was Black, ancestors straight from slavery, I was still visibly Muslim. The more "Islamic" I dressed, the more people would side-eye me. I've had people in waiting rooms get up from their seats and move away. I've had people stare me down, make me feel like nothing. I've had comments made about my hijab, whether or not I was concealing a bomb underneath it. One day, I was asked if I was wearing all black to work because of Osama bin Laden's death.

I once met this girl from the Middle East my freshman year of college. "I didn't know you were Muslim," I said and gave her the Islamic greeting.

"Yeah, it's okay." She shrugged. "My sister and I don't wear it anymore, you know, cuz 9/11."

I nodded. I got it, but then again, I didn't. I wasn't taking off my hijab. Not for other people's ignorance. If I was going to take it off, it'd be because I wanted to. Not because I was pressured by society's ill view of Muslims.

People wear their hijabs (or don't) for many different reasons, but the majority of people, including Becky at the restaurant, believe that it is a universal sign of oppression. The media has made it so that close-minded individuals have been brainwashed to think that when they see a Muslim woman covering her hair and body, it automatically equates with her being forced to by her evil Arabic-speaking father. They have all these notions of you being bald, forced into an arranged marriage, being subservient to a man, and that you absolutely, unequivocally, couldn't be a feminist. All hell would break loose if a hijabi was a feminist.

Deciding, really deciding, to unapologetically wear my hijab for *me* has been the most freeing and rebellious and feminist thing I could possibly do.

I didn't wear my hijab for others, so they could think that I was a good, practicing Muslim. Nah. I did it because it was me, my crown, my shield. It told people that I was strong in my belief, whether I said it or not. I was proud and loud of who I was. And because I was so "out there" with it, it made individuals (like

Becky) very, very uncomfortable. They just couldn't figure out how a girl like me continued to defy odds, being different, being openly true, while getting beat down daily for being a minority Muslim.

I went through a phase when the pressures of being a "poster girl" Muslim got to me. I was visibly hijabi, fat, and Black. I thought that I had something to prove. I wanted acceptance and validation from everyone. Fat girls were seen a certain way, so I needed to dispel those stereotypes. Black girls from Detroit were seen a certain way, so I needed to rise above and be totally non-ghetto, code-switch the hell out of my vocabulary. And Muslims were seen as homophobic extremists. So I had to be cool, and out-of-the-box, and most of all, nonthreatening.

All of that identity shit weighed on me. With all that bending and reshaping, I began to lose a sense of self. I didn't have anyone to let me know that it was perfectly fine to be who the fuck I wanted to be. No one told me that I didn't owe shit to anyone. I didn't have to be a poster child, spokesperson, or representative for any one of the minority groups that I belonged to. I could be me. Unapologetically.

As Muslims, we are taught to be perfect. In front of our peers, in the media, at work, at that nearby coffee shop. We are taught that we are being watched by not only God, but others, and that we need to be amazing individuals who aren't touched by mental illness, sexual abuse, or homosexuality. We've created these ridiculous ideologies that we can only fit nicely into these frames.

I stopped caring about unattainable expectations. I stopped striving for a level of perfection that I was never going to bask in. And every day, I worked on finding me. Not allowing stereotypes to define me.

For one thing, I knew I was Muslim. Wasn't really sure what kind of Muslim I was, but I was Muslim. I knew I was probably always going to be fat. And I couldn't change that I was Black, and I wasn't going to start bleaching and looking like the new

Lil' Kim. So, I swam in the greatness of what those individual things meant to me. They meant originality, they meant power, they meant hope.

■ ■ ■ ■

Before the internet, real-life trolls, aka haters, would shame me. My earliest memory was at the mosque for Friday prayer. When a Muslim makes salat, it is a sacred time, a quiet time; one must not break concentration and one must not talk or touch the person who makes salat. When I knelt down to put my head to the prayer rug, someone, some-fuckin-body, thought that my outfit was obviously not up to prayer standards and proceeded to grab the bottom hem of my shirt and yank it down over my lower back and butt. As you can only imagine, all concentration was lost, and my link to our creator was broken as anger grew around my soul like vines. I wanted to break my prayer and be like, "Which one of y'all touched me?"

Muslims don't show their skin! I imagined one of the old heads saying, once I found out who the culprit was. Needless to say, I never found out who inadvertently policed my body, even during something as sacred as prayer.

My Muslim girl indecencies only grew from there.

I started to wear short sleeves. Was scolded for that. I wore pants instead of skirts. Was scolded for that. I wore sundresses instead of an abaya. Was scolded for that.

Muslim men made me feel the most uncomfortable in my own skin. They'd secretly call me names like "slut" and "whore" and "bitch," because a girl who dressed the way she wanted couldn't have been good news. The interesting thing was that many of them would've slept with me (and a few tried), yet I was all the bad things in the holy book and labeled as a "hoejabi."

I first heard the term "hoejabi" when I was a teenager. A hoejabi wore red lipstick, and with her hijab rocked tight jeans with rips in them exposing her thigh meat. She partied just as hard and went on dates with non-Muslim men. She cussed and did as she pleased. All secretly, of course. A lot of us Muslim women live double lives out of fear of the term, being deemed a hoejabi. Being outed in the community and ostracized for doing the same as men.

I used to be one of those women. Delving into the hoejabi lifestyle, yet checking over my shoulder for brothers in the community in the same damn club waiting to uncover a Muslim sister doing the same wrong as them. One time I was at the club with two of my Muslim girlfriends. It was New Year's Eve. Neither of them wore their scarves, and as for me, I had the most un-Islamic dress on ever. My boobs were out, as well my legs and arms. I gave zero fucks. I just wanted to see what it was like to not be all covered up. In the crowd, one of my friends suddenly pointed, and I ducked when I saw who it was.

"Girl! That's ole dude from the mosque." I grabbed her wrist, trying to pull her into the other direction. "We can't go over there. I don't have any clothes on!"

She rolled her eyes. "It's whatever."

"Fuck," I said under my breath, as I followed behind.

I crossed my arms over my chest trying to maintain some form of modesty, and barely made eye contact as they gave hugs and Islamic greetings.

One of them had alcohol in his hand. "So, what are y'all sisters doing at the club with no scarfs on?"

"What are you doing here in the same club with a drink in your hand?" I cocked my head to the side.

He laughed uncomfortably.

"I'm out," I said, squeezing back into the crowd. At that moment, I knew he was going to go back to the community and tattle on us.

Not only are Islamic communities policing and playing into this one-size-fits-all hijabi stereotype, but the media is as well. Now, folks are confused as to what a real Muslim woman looks like. We've turned the common hijabi into a one-dimensional caricature. And, once again, anyone else who doesn't fit into that mold is quickly discredited, and if we don't shut up, we get trolled and dismissed.

Look around you. The rise of the Instagram hijabi blogger has swept the internet for the last decade. She is usually a size four, her aesthetic is pastels; either she wears her hijab wrapped traditionally or, if she's a little edgy, she may even wear a loosely tied turban that she claims is so cutting-edge, when Africans have been wearing turbans for hundreds of years. She's either a pale Middle Easterner or white-passing, with a hubby with an amazing beard that he obviously conditions weekly cuz like, wow, it's incredibly shiny. He makes corny cameos in her YouTube videos. She has someone take photos of her making salat in a very New York chic way. Can beat her face, travels the world, expenses paid. And bills? What's a bill? Owns a fancy Bengal cat named Sahar. Usually a virgin, even though she has two kids, because Muslim women definitely don't have sex and are just impregnated by sheer will and the divinity of God.

If you look at all the diversity and inclusion campaigns meant to fight against Islamophobia or from companies wanting to jump on them Muslim millennial dollars, you will see the cookie-cutter Muslimah. Tell me, where is the lie here?

As a fat, Black Muslim who definitely doesn't wear pastels and may or may not cuss like someone's disgruntled uncle, I am overlooked. My voice unheard. My stories discredited. And my faith constantly questioned. Muslims as a whole are fighting today for equality and proper representation in the media and within non-Muslim communities. Funny how they seem to forget the in-betweenies, the dark Muslim, the alternative Muslims, and Muslims who are queer. How do you fight for justice for one and not for all?

■ ■ ■ ■

I wouldn't get featured on mainstream hijabi blogs, I suspect, because I'm alternative and I scare the "normal" Muslim. Hell, with as many intersectionalities as I have, I scare most folk. Because of the anti-Blackness and dark-skin color prejudice that is deeply rooted in the Islamic communities, many of these blogs only cater to and highlight acceptable, straight-size, light skin, or white-passing Muslims. So, in response to my annoyance of the current climate and how whitewashed everything was, I directed a photo shoot with an amazing local commercial photographer, Remy Roman. The concept was the Black Panthers, as in the radical group of Black folks in the '70s fighting for Black rights. Of course, a lot of white folks get scared when Black people congregate and ask for equal rights, so the government labeled them as a hate group and disbanded the organization. In homage, I wore all black. Black combat boots, black pants with rips in the knee, black shirt with a pleather jacket, fingerless gloves, and, of course, black lipstick; instead of the Afro, I rocked a hijab, traditionally wrapped.

Although I got seventeen mosquito bites standing in the high grass, the photos were striking. In one photo, I am standing tall and proud with one fist in the air like Tommie Smith and John Carlos did in the 1968 Summer Olympics, when they silently protested the unfair treatment of Blacks in the US.

To my surprise, a popular hijabi blog reposted the photo. There I was, in all of my Black glory in the midst of pale faces in pastels. Then, I held my breath as the comments came in. The first few were iffy, but a slew of other ones were supportive. I tilted my head to the right like a proud mom watching her kid ride a bike for the first time. Then, my notifications started to blow up.

For a full forty-eight hours, I was cyber-bullied, trolled:

She should just take off her hijab!!! She's disgracing Islam.

That's not how Muslim women should dress. She does not represent hijabis.

There's no way she's Muslim.

She's a hoejabi!

Just take the scarf off.

These comments multiplied, as hate always does. Users tagged their friends, and then the nasty comments became a cesspool for body shaming and discrediting my Muslim-ness. Some of them even migrated from the hijabi blog to my personal pages, where I was ridiculed further.

Now, I often get asked how I deal with trolls. There are three levels of trolls. The *ignorant* ones, who may ask a question about my "kind of hijab," which they clearly could've Googled, but I'll respond to them depending on how my day is going and if I want to take the ninety seconds to educate them. The *condescenders*, who try to shame me in a sandwich compliment–type comment, which I delete and block immediately just on the sheer fact that they think I'm just that stupid. The last, the *ballsy commenters*, who usually have no profile photo and under a hundred followers and who have nothing to lose but place the most hateful shit under my photo. For them, I usually delete and block, but once in a while, I'll leave the hate comment up so that my V-Hive (sorry, Beyoncé) can attack.

During that forty-eight-hour period, I ended up deleting and blocking hundreds of hate comments. It was a record for me. The comments even made me question my Islam and how I choose to share it with the world. I couldn't help but pause and feel periodic shame. Perhaps some of those trolls had a point. Maybe I should just take off my hijab.

I've always loved Islam for the peace that it gives me, its mediation components, and the constant reiteration of hope and forgiveness. I love the sisterhood aspect and how giving Muslims are. But there have been moments in my life when I didn't want to be involved with Islam anymore. Not because of the religion itself but because of the politics of the people who seem to have claimed it as theirs. They've taken Islam out of context and have force-fed it to its congregations. And mostly to its girls and women. Many will argue that these instances of toxic masculinity and oppression don't happen in the States, that this is a foreign Muslim issue, but it's not. I've witnessed it.

At a young age, I started noticing the difference in how Muslim girls were treated versus Muslim boys. Young girls' roles were in the home. As for the boys, they were allowed to roam free, make mistakes, explore, and get away with certain acts. They were barely ever questioned, if even questioned at all. When girls wanted to go out, they'd be questioned. Asked all the details of where they were going, who they were going with, and given a time to be back. If they strayed from anything, then punishment would follow. I watched girls made to do house chores and clean up after their male siblings, when the males had no assigned household duties. Girls were watched like hawks, no privacy at all, as the boys flew under the radar. We were prepped to remain virgins, get married, obey, be a good Muslim, have kids, pray, and smile. While the boys got to explore their sexuality and hide porn under their beds and talk to non-Muslim girls on the phone.

One wrong move and a Muslim girl's name could be tarnished in the community. As for the boys, well, boys will be boys. This type of mentality has made many Muslim men from where I come from very toxic, controlling, messy, and abusive. For every Muslim woman who tiptoes on eggshells, there is her male counterpart fucking up with no sense of accountability.

Many people may disagree with my analysis and tell me that I'm adding to Islamophobia, that I am making Muslims look bad. But remember that this is my truth and what I've witnessed growing up in a Black, Muslim community. Trust me when I tell you that I wish I hadn't grown up around toxic masculinity and overt oppression.

These types of "hush, hush" Muslims are what's wrong with the community. They only wish to highlight the good and sweep the bad under the rug as to keep up appearances. What they fail to understand is that by creating this perfect Muslim character, they are doing more damage than good. Muslim women aren't allowed to truly explore themselves or their sexuality without someone smacking their hand and saying, "Nu-uh-uhhhh. *Haram!*"

Religion and spirituality are such personal things, but it seems like in today's judgmental era that I have to prove how Muslim I am. In order to be a good Muslim, I have to show the world how I practice.

■ ■ ■ ■

I was in a private hot tub with one of my good friends who also happens to be Muslim. In the water, she wore her scarf tied in the back, a short-sleeve shirt, and leggings. I wore a long-sleeved bathing suit with no scarf. I just didn't want to wear it that day.

I posted a boomerang of the upper half of my body in the water doing a peace sign online, and I immediately got a private message:

Hey, umm, are you like not Muslim anymore? I'm a Muslim and I follow your page because I love that you promote inclusion in Islam and I really admire your style, but I didn't follow you to see you without a scarf on and did you know that men can see you?

When I tell you that I gagged, I gagged. The message was so problematic that I couldn't even do anything but block the fuck out of her. I wish you could have seen how hard I pressed my finger on that block button.

First of all—when a Black woman says "first of all," then you know a read is coming—I wanted to know, why does my hijab equate with Muslim-ness? So, there aren't Muslims who don't wear hijab? Are they not still Muslim? And whether my hijab is on or off, my choice by the way, what does it matter to you? Does each time a Muslim in the world decides to not wear hijab, does a part of your arm start stinging? Am I causing you immense pain to look at my tiny blonde Afro?

The last part angered me the most. The "men can see you" part. Umm, yeah, I know. And if they don't want to see all of this body, then I recommend them either closing their eyes or turning away. I'm not dressing for men. Been there and done that. Men's eyes don't dictate what I put on my body. Period.

From a young age, growing up Muslim, particularly growing up as a Muslim girl, meant I had to conceal, to lower my gaze, to be pure and soft and quiet. It was to float on water like I was some damn deity with my silk hijab and loose-fitted garments just angelically trailing behind me. Sins. What sins? I was a pious Muslimah. And I was not seen as human.

A few misogynistic Muslim men, including my ex, love saying this quote to get their wives and daughters to stay in their place: *it says that more women will be in the hellfire than men.* Ha! About 90 percent of the world is run by men, and some pretty fucked-up stuff has occurred while men have been in charge. I'm gonna take a wild guess and say that that's debatable. But listen, I'm no scholar.

Because of how the world views Islam and the misrepresentation in the media, a lot of people blame Islam for the inequalities I face. So-called feminists and rights groups love outing Muslim women. I've seen signs that read: *Islam = Oppression* and *hijab ban.* What they've done in return is become the oppressor that they are so against. You are telling me that my hijab oppresses me and that I cannot be Muslim and be a feminist. Bullshit.

Not only are Muslims oppressed by their own but by society as well. Don't tell a Muslim woman what she can and cannot be.

This may be an unpopular opinion, but the Quran contains verses on feminist acts. Our beloved prophet's wife owned an entire business. Women are given rights and access to education, told not to be oppressed. The man who oppresses a woman gets punished. There's another verse that says that heaven lies at the foot of a mother. Muslim men love to blame feminism and female empowerment as the cause of our rising divorce rates and family dysfunctions, while twisting the words of the holy book to their own advantage. We call the male version of Islam, "Hislam." Get it? His Islam.

I always find it funny how my own people troll me the most, but Muslim men seem to be my biggest non-fan fans. They hate that I am carefree, that I am not controllable and not easily persuaded. Yet, it still turns them on.

They are the ones that troll hijabi influencers from the crypts of their mother's basements, claiming that the tightness of our dresses is ruining the very fabric of Islam and that they must save us by eradicating feminism, but these are the very men that slide into "hoejabis" inboxes with hairy ass dick pics from 1972 and requests to see our boobs and vaginas. Fetishizing and objectifying our bodies. But we are the problems.

By now, I have been attacked personally through every medium you can think of. Trolled by white supremacists who told me to "go back where I came from" for standing in solidarity with Colin Kaepernick when he knelt during the national anthem. Fat-shamed by thin folk who just "care about my health." And other hijabis that tell me that my turban is not "real hijab."

Overall, I think I do a pretty good job at dealing with hatred.

But one day, a mega-troll warrior entered into my realm with his sword drawn, and I was completely caught off guard. It was a hot summer morning, and I was in my bed in front of the fan talking shit on the internet, per usual. I got a private Facebook message. My eyes darted back and forth like a detective. I'm always wary of private messages now. I tapped on the notification and scanned the message. It was from a girl I knew online. A Pakistani activist.

HER: I just want you to know that you are so incredible and the work that you are doing is needed. Don't ever stop. Like ever. No matter what anyone says. You are gorgeous and a force to be reckoned with.

ME: *Tongue pop* I knoooooo right.

HER: I'm sorry to tell you this, buuuut there's a man that started an IG page to attack you.

ME: *Deep sighs* Honestly, I don't even care because I literally can't deal with it right now. If I look at the dumb shit, I know I'm gonna be triggered.

HER: I totes understand. I won't even show it to you.

ME: Good.

I nibbled on my bottom lip in annoyance, as I usually do when faced with foolishness. I told myself, nope not today. He will not ruin my day. I will not look at it. It is not worth my time. Fuck him and the computer he uses.

Bad news spreads quickly on the internet. Two more women in-boxed me, alerting me that a man was belittling influential hijabis. Using our images to sexually degrade and mock us. This time around, I bit my lip a little harder to where it stung. I don't usually address trolls because that's what they want. They want their three seconds of notoriety, doesn't matter if it's negative. They project their own insecurities, then it turns into full-blown hatred and jealousy.

Stop being a pussy and look, I said to me. How bad could it actually be?

I clicked on his profile. To my dismay, he had been using my full-body pic as his profile photo. I lifted my head to the sky. The fucker didn't even give me proper credit! In his bio, it said, "Before you report me, watch all my vids." His hate page had about six hundred followers. I lost faith in internet humanity. Through my faux FBI training, I could tell it was a fairly new hate page because he only had six videos up. I immediately saw mine. But to lessen the blow, I opted to watch the one before mine.

It was disgusting. What he'd done was steal photos from our pages, animate them, and place his voice over the animations. In the first video, he used a popular Middle Eastern hijabi model and ridiculed her chin shape; in his voice, and he tried hard to sound like a lady, he asked users to "cum on her face."

The anger welled up inside me as I finished the videos and read the comment section. Future note to self: never read the comment section. The vid had thousands of views. People ridiculed her and planted laughing emojis, egging cyberbullying, and hate rhetoric. Had they not known that the women he made fun of were real people?

I had to watch mine next. He had taken the photo from Paris that I had been very proud of. The one where I had just been divorced for six months and finally felt good about myself. The one where I am half bent over, my derriere against the wall with a Parisian-looking hat, being oh-so high fashion.

He used that dumb-ass lady voice again, pretending that it was mine. Mocking me. He made fun of how fat I was and said that I would die from diabetes. How dumb my feminist movement was. He said that I wasn't really empowering anyone at all. Then he ended the animation with a fireball poop emoji coming out of my butt and blowing everything up.

I found myself sitting with a mix of emotions, one being discomfort and the other, doubt. I just couldn't believe that he had followed me, had access to my feed, then took one of my photos, and literally sat for hours animating, recording, and editing a full hate video. I was low-key honored and, on the other hand, scared. How long had he planned this? Obsessed about how to top all the trolls I've ever come across. I felt violated. And there was nothing I could do. I had no face to connect the nastiness to, a cyber-ghost.

I hated that this stranger made me feel like I had done something wrong by putting my fat, Muslim body on display. He tapped into my insecurity of not being worthy enough to take up space. For so long, I hadn't thought I deserved space unless I was thin and white like Becky with the good hair.

How could I fight back? I was only one influencer . . . with a whole community behind her.

I took the photo he stole, posted it, and tagged him. I told people what he said about me and other Muslim women. The outrage spun into solidarity, as my followers added him, in-boxed him, and reported his page and all his subpar animation attempts. Hundreds of gals reported him. Sent me messages of support. Told me that my work was important. That I was important. Instagram kept sending reporters messages saying that he had not violated any of their hate terms, even though he had clearly used content without authorization.

But we kept at it despite the roadblocks. In forty-eight hours, Instagram finally took down his page. It was a feminist victory.

Of course, he reappeared on another page. Since I had blocked him, another one of my faux FBI followers followed the case closely and monitored his new whereabouts. She said he had ended up doing a live video. He was a twenty-five-year-old Muslim man living in the US. In the video, he said he made the animations to stop online hijabis from messing up the religion.

I gagged. So, in his warped mind, he thought that belittling and sexually fetishizing women and their bodies was going to force us into Islamic submission? He had also been known for harassing hijabis on their own pages and trolling countless other accounts.

This isn't the last time something like this will happen to me and others like me. As I climb the ladder of—well, whatever the ladder is that I'm climbing—more hate will spill out people's fingers and through the World Wide Web. But it's okay. I've been through some major shit in my life, and the patriarchy won't ever stop this train.

14. LIFE IN THE DAY OF A FAT MODEL

I went to Big Sister's house to pick up my mail. I hadn't planned on living in Detroit for this long and instead of switching my address eighty times, I kept it in one spot until I got my shit together. It'd been almost two months, and I'd been waiting for my first modeling check to come. Every day, I'd text her and ask her if it came. I'd hear her eyes rolling over the phone, followed by a no, not yet.

Then boom! It arrived. I couldn't hide my excitement as I carefully tore open the envelope to make sure the three zeros were there, followed by the one. With tears welling in my eyes, I began to laugh uncontrollably, still with the check in hand.

"What's so funny?" Big Sis leaned in my passenger side window with a burgundy bath towel on her head, shielding her upper body from the blazing sun.

"People are actually paying my fat ass to model." I wiped my eyes with the back of my hand. "I'm short. My teeth aren't straight. I'm Black and I'm Muslim. I can't even walk in heels."

I remembered painstakingly dialing up AOL and looking up the standards for modeling. Every single agency from New York to LA required their models to be at least five feet eight and between the sizes of zero and eight. Long legs. Giraffe necks. Most of them were pale too. But legally, I don't think they could say they were only looking for white-white models.

Only a few of them had plus-size divisions. My mouth watered. For sure, I'd be able to fit into that category. Wrong. Still had to be tall and statuesque, with a tad bit more meat, but only in the right places. They wanted sizes eight to fourteen, and the gag was they had to be "proportionate." I was about one hundred pounds too big and seventy inches too short. I could lose weight. To get to a size six from a twenty-four would require immediate death. I'd have to be dead for at least forty days or so to drop the unwanted poundage; then maybe if I was a good Muslim and I prayed super-duper hard, God would resurrect me like Jesus. A thinner, more model-esque Jesus. I had only one other problem. My height. I had been a dorky kid, so I knew all kinds of interesting facts. I had heard through the grapevine that in order to gain a few inches of height, Asians were having doctors break their kneecaps and then fusing some extra bone, cartilage, whatever, and that when they healed, they were three to four inches taller than before. I was already five foot four, so it'd be perfect.

The practice wasn't legal in the States, so I'd have to travel to Asia. I could stop spending my chore money on the ice cream truck and 7-Eleven slushies and put that money to better use. The last step was recovery from them breaking my bones. I thought about my pain tolerance and how I had fractured, not broken, but fractured my tibia that last summer, and how much pain I was in and kiddie depression. For eight weeks, I wore a misshapen and smelly cast. If I went through with the procedure, I'd have to wear not one but two misshapen and smelly casts.

This wasn't going to work.

I gave up and embraced the thought that I'd never be pretty and that I'd never be a model like Tyra Banks, until an online friend living in New York told me that she'd gotten an email from an agency looking for hijabi models and that I should apply.

Ha! I said to myself. I'd never get chosen by an agency. Do you know how many models are in New York already? How many pastel-wearing, perfect-Instagram-life, hijabi bloggers were already there that'd beat me in followers and picture quality? I'm too raw. Untamed. I mean, I am fierce but New York fierce, I think not.

ME: Girl, they'd never pick me.
HER: Apply anyway
ME: *Cyber rolls eyes*

I was sitting in my office, and by office, I mean bed with two worn pillows propped behind my back and another pillow and folded blanket that works as a makeshift laptop desk. I clicked on the link she had sent, and it led me to an agency website and application to fill out for the position. I giggled the entire time as I typed in my measurements and height and added a few flattering photos.

What's the harm in trying?

Submit.

Early the next day, I checked my email as I usually do while drinking spicy apple cider vinegar tea and speed-eating oatmeal, which I absolutely hate, but eat anyway because oatmeal is good for you and it takes a second to make.

The agency had emailed me back in less than twelve hours after I sent in my app. Clearly, they had been so disgusted with my disproportionate measurements that they thought it was fitting to reject me on the spot. I got it. I wasn't everyone's cup of tea with a splash of almond milk.

My eyes scanned over it, in search for the fuck you, you're very ugly, and never apply for anything remotely like this ever again in your life. Instead, they used phrases like "our client loves you" and "we are pleased" and "are you available Tuesday?"

Gulping down the last bit of oatmeal, I messaged my friend.

ME: Girl, why this scam ass agency talking about some they love my look. Ha! Sounds like a scam to me.
HER: Scam? That's a legit company. I've worked with them before.

ME: Huh?

HER: That's a real company, boo boo. You got it!!!

Still in disbelief, I emailed the supposed agency girl back and asked which company would I be so-called "modeling" for?

She responded, "Refinery 29."

I couldn't help but think that somehow I had scammed them into believing I was worthy enough to model for them, that they'd find out that I was fatter than my photos showed, and that they'd toss me off the set as soon as I walked through the door. I was a small-time model from Detroit without an agent. I mean, I had modeled in Paris and LA, but those were smaller gigs that I had set up myself. Oh, and I had modeled for Adidas Originals, too, but I could barely fit into their stuff. New York was intimidating. They'd expect me to be on the entire time. What if my IBS acted up, I shitted in their fancy schmancy clothes, and ruined the whole shoot? What if I died on the way there and they'd be like, "Ugh, I knew her fat ass would so die on the way here. Such a typical fattie." And worse, what if I couldn't fit into any of their wardrobe?

The team and I emailed back and forth about what I could and couldn't wear due to being a covered Muslimah. Then we got into sizing. The agency gave me the stylist's Instagram, so I could see who'd I be working with. The head stylist was that typical tan, privileged, and thin white girl with even whiter teeth and soft brown tresses with honey blonde highlights. She's possibly never seen cellulite in her life. She'd probably vomit seeing mine. I'd been on a set before, and I'd have to be naked during fittings and outfit changes. I knew the drill. Beads of sweat rolled down my neck as I anticipated the judgment.

I sent in my size and measurements. She replied: "Great. Do me a favor and just bring in some of your fave outfits."

I sighed. I read that again as: "Whoa. You are super big. Bigger than we thought. Please, bring your own shit cuz clearly we can't accommodate all that bawdy."

I responded: "Will do."

The day of the shoot, I woke up super-early to hit the musty streets and lugged my entire life in a large piece of luggage down and up eight hundred steps before I reached the headquarters of R29, forty-five minutes late.

It was surreal to be standing there. Me. A broke bitch from Detroit. The girl whose dreams were to model in the Big Apple and even thought about breaking her kneecaps just to have a spot among the elite.

Just life in the day of a fat model.

I struggled through the revolving doors with my huge bag that almost dislocated my shoulder as it got stuck on the way around. I pretended nothing happened, then waltzed up to the security counter. I announced, "I'm here to model for Refinery 29."

The guard who had a high weave pony tail and long red nails looked at me like I was crazy and tapped the sign-in sheet. She then held up a mini-camera and pointed it at my face. "Smile," she said with minimal lip movement or any other facial expression. I smiled wide. The light flashed. Seconds later, a sticky badge came from the printer. She slid it to me. "Straight to the elevators. Thirty-ninth floor."

So high up, I noted, like some tourist.

The elevator doors dinged and separated from one another. I felt like a Black Carrie Bradshaw stepping out. R29 had an entire two floors just for their offices. I was shook. In front of two huge glass doors was the company logo in yellow and pink and red. I pulled out my phone, and as I tried to take a photo, some workers passed me. I casually pretended to be texting someone. I didn't want them to think I was new to this type of stuff. Like I'd never been on the thirty-ninth floor of a fancy building in New York that held large media companies or whatever. When the door shut behind them, I took a photo and posted it to the 'Gram with the caption "Guess where I am, bitches?"

Finally, I stepped in for my meeting. The head stylist that I had cyber-stalked greeted me at the door. I have this thing that I do when I don't feel very confident, or inadequate; I act like the most confident person in the room. I pretend to be the woman that I want to be. That I see making deals and not taking shit or no for an answer. I lift my head higher and strut with purpose.

She greeted me and took me to a back area that was our set for the day.

There was a huge vanity mirror with those bubble-looking lights trailing each side, exactly as I had seen in white movie-star movies. By it were two tall makeup chairs, one empty and in the other, another hijabi model and a makeup artist dusting her face with translucent powder. In the next corner was a window that covered half of the wall. From it, I was able to see little people below hustling to their next appointment; across was a glass building just as tall as the one we were in. The sun glistened on the structure, making it look like crystals. Next was a tall rack of clothes and tables filled with posh shades and necklaces and designer scarves. The shoes. They were made of satin and probably real leather, and clunky heels lined the racks. The last table was filled with breakfast foods: croissants, blueberry muffins, chocolate chip cookies, purple and green grapes, and Fiji Water.

The table of sugary carbs had gone untouched, because the room was full of very thin white girls, each equipped with tall Starbucks coffees. Probably skim. Or maybe almond because that's like, ya know, in.

Although I was starving after the long haul with my luggage, I wasn't going to be the first one to dig into that muffin tray. Plus, I still wasn't sure how the clothes would fit, so I needed to be as thin-fat as possible. One bite of muffin could easily take me from a size twenty-four to thirty-two in a snap.

The stylist showed me to my rack of clothes and the makeshift dressing area they created. One of the stylists had on low-riders and a little tee. I could see her hip bones peeking out whenever she twisted her torso or reached for something on the top of the something. I wondered if I had any hip bones or if it was just a thin-person thing. The world may never know.

My thoughts were quickly interrupted when she asked about the items I brought from home. I handed her the luggage, and she began to sift through my array of big-girl clothes. I imagined her judging me, but perhaps that was my own insecurity.

The other girl handed me the first outfit. The white girl was so excited, so I smiled like a good person and retreated behind the black curtain.

The dress was gorgeous. I held it up to admire its full beauty. I checked the tag. It was by a designer I didn't know. I wondered how much it cost. And I was excited that I was actually allowed to wear something that probably cost as much as my rent. Every time I try on clothes, I stretch the item out as far as I can across my body and eye it. Hmm, maybe this part will fit? I also do the same to the inside of the sleeve. I use my hands to stretch and test the width. Sleeves are always an issue for me. My arms were basically donated to me by none other than a sumo wrestler. We have big arms in my family. It's genetic. It's problematic for jackets and shirts.

The back of my neck itched. I placed the dress down carefully and removed my clothes in front of the full-body mirror. I had gotten down to my Walmart bra that had seen better days and a pair of clean yet dingy panties.

Before I put the dress over my head, I called upon my Lord. I pinched my eyes shut and spoke with him directly: *Allah, if you are listening, I need you. I know you have far better things to do, but in my hand, I hold a dress that has sleeves that do not stretch. I'm shook. If you could intervene in some way, that'd be cool. Ameen.*

I poked my head through the opening. *Bam!* It went through. I sucked my stomach in as if that was going to help what happened next. One arm in. The other arm in. The bottom of the dress fell to the floor. I was in it. But I was stuck. The sleeves were so tight that I couldn't even drop them. I looked like a bold, human letter "T."

"Leah?" Skinny girl number two asked. "How's everything going?"

"Umm." I quietly jumped up and down trying to loosen the death lock that the sleeves had on my arms. I wanted to cry so bad. I was stuck. I admitted after the seconds that passed felt like hours, "I, uh, think I'm stuck."

She pulled back the curtain, and with her hand on her hip, she tapped her chin in deep thought. "I think it looks gorgeous."

The other girl followed and started tugging at the fabric. "Can you put your arms down?"

My eyes shifted. "I can't."

"Well, you just need to open up the arms a bit." She searched around the table.

"What? How?"

She lifted a pair of scissors. "Just cut a little opening in the back."

"Wait, you're going to cut this fancy dress?"

She pinched the fabric and started snipping away. "Don't move."

My worst fear came true. Not only not being able to fit into a garment but then being stuck in it. And now my body became the "special project" for these thin girls who probably had their own body image issues but would never know what it was like to feel the humiliation of being a fattie in a thin-obsessed world.

I wondered how she and the rest of the gals in that room felt as they saw her cutting holes in the back of my sleeves so that my fat could breathe.

The negative possibilities spun out of control as I questioned my own weight and size. If I were twenty pounds smaller, then I could fit into this beautiful piece; if I were smaller, then I wouldn't have had to bring my entire wardrobe, unlike the other straight-size model. *They hadn't asked her to bring anything. They were afraid that I wouldn't be able to fit into anything, and they just wanted to safeguard themselves against having a plus-size model with absolutely no clothes. You could be small like them, if you just stopped eating. If you just stopped needing food. If you started to weigh yourself obsessively like you had a long time ago. Maybe diet culture ain't that toxic. Maybe you should skip all meals for the rest of the day. You don't deserve to eat.*

She had finished cutting the long slits. "There, just don't take any photos from the back." She giggled.

I pulled a smile from my bag and gave it to her. I turned my back to the mirror and saw my arm fat hanging out of the sleeves like the dough from a busted can of Pillsbury biscuits. The humiliation was real. And I had to walk the streets of New York like that.

As a plus model, I'm not usually self-conscious, but that day, I was throttled back into a very destructive time. A time where I heavily policed my body, and every single thing that went into my mouth. Where I avoided mirrors, avoided photos. Sat with my stomach tucked in and ordered Diet Cokes instead of real meals.

And this was only outfit number one. With each shirt or pair of pants, I would hold my breath, just praying that I could squeeze in somehow, and just pray that I was skinny. I'd be wondering if she'd have to literally cut every item that I wore and have to watch as the other model had not one issue wearing all the clothes she was given. The ease of working with a small person. After me, they'd never want to work with another fat model again. How many plus-size models would I have ruined it for?

We took an Uber XL to location number one. How ironic that it was a popular doughnut shop. In the first shot, they wanted us to sit on the stools and pretend to drink coffee and eat doughnuts. I couldn't take full advantage of my angles because I didn't want to the slits to show.

Leah, you are fuckin' up this entire shoot!

Why had they even wasted their time choosing me?

You are just not cut out for this.

We finished the group shots. Now they wanted individuals. "You can go first," I told the other model. I needed time to get my head right and had about three minutes.

I obsessed over why they had chosen me in the first place out of the hundreds if not thousands of New York–based hijabi models. What made me special? I wasted half of my three minutes trying to put together a conclusion that really didn't matter. Why had it mattered that I was chosen and they weren't? All that mattered was that I *was* chosen. The universe aligned for that opportunity to literally fall into my lap. Who was I to question the universe? The universe was like, hey, take this shit, and shoved this opportunity in my arms, and there I was complaining about having to fancily prance around New York City with the backs of my fat arms out. I was having a spoiled rich kid moment without the rich part. I was thirty, old as fuck by modeling industry standards. I was Black. Not light-skinned biracial Black, but Black-Black. Muslim and fat. I had a short neck and stumpy legs with bad knees.

I had thirty seconds left of my mini get-right session, and the humiliation dissipated as I thought about all the girls and women who would see these photos of my double chin, needed to see an underdog pursuing modeling in an industry that's usually thin and white or the right kind of curvy. For people who had never been considered beautiful or worthy or just never fit in.

I deserved to be there. To stand there among those Starbucks Barbies in all of my fat, Black glory. And I was going to be the fiercest they've ever seen, paving the way for other fatties pursuing modeling.

"Leah," the photographer said. "It's your turn."

"Here." I handed the assistant my bag without waiting for her response, like one of those rich Caucasians being a rich Caucasian. "I'm ready."

I harnessed the modeling power angles of Muva Naomi, the catlike fierceness of Tyra, and the predrug carefreeness of Janice Dickinson.

We shot for eight hours in nine different locations and three outfit changes. Not all the clothes they gave me fit or looked good. The second-to-last outfit was flat-out ugly and shapeless. I stuck up for myself and said that I wasn't feeling that particular one.

She changed it. I stood in front of them in bra and panties and hairy underarms.

I finally ate. I was even the first one in line for lunch. And those chocolate chip cookies, I had three of them. They were good too.

At the end of the day, she told me that the photos were going to be used as stock photos for R29's social media and affiliated websites. I didn't care where they put them, just as long as it wasn't some fetish Muslim porn site. Other than that, I was getting paid for the first time since Paris and London, and I was just excited to have money coming in.

I had no expectation for them to, like, blow up or anything.

A month later, the photos were released in conjunction with International Muslim Women's Day. That morning, I started getting texts of screenshots of my face from all over. They were on all of R29's feeds and MTV.com, and they even animated me and put me on Snapchat's discovery page with real-life celebs.

After I got over all of my "ohhhmagah" moments, I sat back in my old creaky chair and with my hands behind my head, I told myself, "Just another day in the life of a fat model."

15. MUSLIM GIRL DANCE

"**S**o, what's your angle here?" the photographer asked.

"Well," I said flipping my hijab and popping my tongue. "I want this to be super easy. The angle is just a carefree, fat Muslim girl dancing in the streets while simultaneously being a bad-ass boss bitch. But most importantly, I love the idea of body acceptance through doing something as vulnerable as dancing. And I want there to be a bit of spoken word. Can you make this happen?"

"Got it. What kind of choreography will you be doing?" She leaned in.

I pouted. "None. It's a freestyle-type thing. Wing it. Ya know."

Her brows crinkled.

"Don't worry. I got this. I dance all the time. You've seen me busting moves at the club before."

She burst out laughing and hit the table. "Okay!"

The waiter set two bowls of pho on the table.

As she slurped noodles and broth, she asked, "Why do this video now?"

"Well, I've come to terms with people, society, my own being uncomfortable with my body. Seeing a body like mine taking up space is something people need to see. Because discomfort is growth, right?"

"I totally agree," she said and looked over to her husband.

He smiled and nodded. I took that as a go. We were making an official dance video.

"Oh, I just wanted to add that if this video does well, we will be getting a lot of hate."

She grimaced. "What? Why?"

"Because the masses don't like it when people like me live in my truth. We will get hate from fat-shamers. Extremist Muslims. Men who live in deep dark basement dungeons who troll fabulous fat women in their unlimited spare time, and whoever else doesn't agree with unconventional bodies living unapologetically."

∎ ∎ ∎ ∎

It was humid that evening. Ninety degrees. On top of being nervous, since I hadn't rehearsed anything, I was horrified. *You are gonna fuck this up and waste their time.* Then the *gurgle-gurgle* followed. For some reason, I was always getting myself into positions like this. I'd have all these grand dreams and schemes, and then the day came, and I was frozen. What the hell? I wasn't even a real dancer. I mean, I could twerk and stuff, but that's not what I was going to do for the whole video. It wasn't even a twerk video. Muslim girl twerks! No. The internet was going to skin me alive. I'd be turned into memes. Not the cute ones but the offensive ones. There was so much on my body that they could make fun of. Like a plethora of things. I was a mega-troll's dream.

The first shot was me in hijab with a hat on with gold lettering and a black jacket and leggings. This was going to be my speaking part before the dancing commenced. The camera would zoom in from far away and then stop right at my face. My cameo: do I make you uncomfortable?

Easy peasy. Basically just like regular modeling but with one line. Just one line, I told myself. *Gurgle-gurgle.*

I rolled my eyes.

"Action!"

Give 'em attitude.

My makeup artist patted my face down with extra powder. I was melting, and I hadn't even started dancing yet.

The next location was the corner of a busy intersection. Great, now I had to dance in front of passing cars and people on the sidewalk. I wondered if there was an available yet private alley we could utilize.

"Okay," she turned up the music on her iPhone. "And action."

I danced hard. The hardest I'd ever danced. *One-two. One-two. Boomcat. Boomcat. Ah. Ah. Ah. Hit it.* For the entire song, I moved to the beat for a full minute and a half while her husband went around me with his expensive camera.

The song ended. I was out of breath. "Was that good?" I huffed.

"Great." She gave me a thumbs-up. "Now do that again but over here by that building."

I'd have to do that multiple times over a two-hour period. Oh, boy.

During each take, people would try to jump in the shots. Dance behind me or with me. I was so hyper-focused on hitting the moves that I wasn't bothered. My friend would try and shoo them away or grab them before they could ruin the shot. People driving by would honk or yell out the window. A few slowed down and hung out their windows. One even parked to watch the dancing unfold. My stomach left me alone, and I was shooting my little dance video.

On the last take, a group of guys were walking down the sidewalk. One asked, "Wow, is she a celebrity?"

My friend smiled. "Almost."

The day came when the video was supposed to be released. The photographer sent it to me at 6:30 p.m. The day was nearly over. I had just been walking back to my car, when I got her text and watched the entire video.

The entire video was almost two minutes. It was good. But not spectacular like her other videos. And my spoken-word part was not included. The video appeared to have been pieced together at the last minute. I was mortified and confused.

ME: Hey! Where's the spoken-word part? Is this the finished video or . . . ?

HER: Leah, it's the complete video. I wasn't able to sync the music to your spoken-word portion, so I made the executive decision to cut that part.

My eyes rolled back so far. She made an executive decision? On my video? Girrrrrrrll. The spoken-word part was the second-most important part. And if that was the case, why hadn't she talked to me about it when I texted her leading up to the release?

I've learned early on to choose my words wisely when I'm expressing some kind of disdain and to be hyperaware of how assertive I am in the workplace, ya know, since Black girls are always being deemed ghetto and loud and angry. But had I been a man doing the same thing, I'd be direct, a go-getter, knows what he wants, and has great leadership qualities. For someone like me to thrive, I have to play the part of agreeable, less intimidating Black girl.

ME: The spoken-word part is very important to me. And I think my followers would really enjoy not only the dancing but my words as well. If you need more time to edit, we can postpone the release date.

HER: I personally think that the video is amazing without the spoken-word part.

I clenched my fist.

ME: I can't release an incomplete video. So, if you need more time that's cool.

HER: Leah, are you saying that I half-assed your video? I thought we were better than that. I'd never, ever do something like that for a paid or volunteered project.

ME: I never said you half-assed it. But the video isn't what we discussed.

She ignored me. I gave her some time to cool off, since she was obviously upset. Maybe she was overwhelmed with all the projects she was working on. I got it. But she could've told me that instead of volunteering for a video with an already full schedule. A wise woman said: Never mix business and friendship.

And I had done just that.

I soon texted her again, asking when she'd have time to reedit the video. She gave me a date of two weeks. I waited. Two weeks passed. I texted her again and asked. She said next week. Nothing. I texted her again. Finally, she said she wasn't editing it again and that if she had to send it out to her intern, that he'd charge me.

Wow.

Weeks after, I texted her and said that I wanted to speak with her in person because I didn't want this video to break up our friendship, and she ignored me. And that was that.

I had an incomplete video and a lost friendship.

Afterward, I'd heard through the grapevine that she claimed that I was being a "diva," that I was "difficult to work with." I thought that was funny because all I asked her to do was what she said, what she volunteered to do in the first place.

There was something deeper going on around that time though. I was beginning to gain notoriety, and she, as well as a few other mutual friends, started acting distant. When I told them in the group chat that I was getting into *Elle* magazine, I was met with underlying animosity. They claimed that I was hiding events from them. Perhaps they thought that I believed that I was better than them. If they had believed that, then it was only their own insecurities. Something that I couldn't have possibly saved.

Summer came and went, and I would periodically be reminded of my failed attempt at a dance video as followers would inquire about it. I'd always say technical difficulties but be super-mad about it.

"Why don't you just release it anyway?" A friend asked.

"No!"

She scoffed, "Why?"

"Cuz it's not what I want."

"Well, can you find another editor?"

"I'm broke."

"Oh, yeah."

"You know how to edit a little."

"I mean, I guess."

The teaser video they had made had a bit of spoken word in it. And the other video had the dancing. OMG. I could edit the two together and release it. It wasn't a hundred, but it was something.

So, four months later, I released my video and titled it "Muslim Girl Dance."

People were sharing and reposting and commenting. It was nuts.

The first week, it hadn't gone viral like I thought it would. But I was proud that I had made it. I didn't have to go viral to be important. The work I did was important, whether or not people saw it.

The next week, I was getting emails for interviews. The video was featured on *Huffington Post*, CBS, CBC, Yahoo, Bustle, and countless other media outlets. After all of those interviews and features, the video went semi-viral, garnering a quarter-million views. My friend who works for a huge AM news station texted me and asked if I'd like to come on her show to talk about the video. Fuck yeah, I typed.

The newsroom was huge. There were IT geeks and reporters everywhere. There were multiple recording studios too. It was legit. We took the last studio, and although I was nervous, my friend eased my mind. And I didn't even have to poop. The interview was about fifteen minutes. We removed our headphones, and she told me that she'd post the audio as well as the video itself.

When it was ready, she texted me the link. I shared it as I usually do, but I hadn't listened to it because I hate the way my voice sounds. The very next day, there was a spike in my blog views. I clicked the link to see where all the traffic was coming from. There were like hundreds of unique visitors. And they were all reading about the "Muslim Girl Dance" video blog post. I figured out that they had come from CBS. My story had made it to the cover page. Right at the top. FAT. BLACK. And MUSLIM. In huge letters. OMG. This is nuts. A refined website like CBS chose my story as the top. I was shooketh.

I got tons of love. At first. Then the trolls started.

The comments underneath the story on CBS's page were derogatory. Luckily, there were only a few. I could take a few. It chipped at my feelings, but I had gotten hate comments before, so I was prepared for it.

Twenty-four hours passed, and I woke up to too many notifications. They had found all of my social media handles and were tag-teaming me. On my blog, I had comments of how disgusting I looked dancing. On Facebook were comments about how I was promoting obesity and how I should just kill myself. That my body made people want to vomit. But the YouTube comments took the cake. Not only was my body under attack, but they attacked my hijab. I was told by a Muslim man that he hoped "Allah breaks my back, so that I couldn't dance ever again." I was told that a Muslim woman should never wear as much makeup as me. That I was an embarrassment to Muslims all over the world. That I should just take my hijab off. And that I was not a Muslim.

The harassment lasted for a full forty-eight hours. The comments got so frequent that I had to turn off my notifications on my phone and laptop. My friends and followers tried to clap back. I told them not to. That they'd just come harder. I kept getting texts and screenshots. I told them to stop sending them. I was triggered. The interesting thing is that most of the hate came from males—Muslim and non-Muslim. For some reason, the freeness of my body and religion in the video was a personal attack on them, somehow, some way.

■　■　■　■

In the mornings, I have this ritual. I juice fruits and veggies. Drink that nasty shit down real quick. I make instant oatmeal. That shit is nasty too. I put butter and allspice in it to make it semi-edible. I boil water and put in two spoonfuls of organic apple cider vinegar, honey, and lemon. I drink it with my nasty oatmeal. Then I check my emails, which I hate doing.

It was the end of September when I got an email from the head of the Women's Studies Department at the University of Ottawa. She said she'd seen my dance video on *Huffington Post* and wanted to fly me out to the Muslim Women: Identities, Labels, and Live Experiences Event.

I laughed. My mouth full of half-chewed oatmeal. Someone all the way in Canada wanted to fly me out? So, I Googled her name—Dr. Ummni Khan. She was, in fact, the head of the department. She was real. I was going to fuckin' Canada.

I was scared as hell to fly to Canada. Ever since I had been denied entrance one time a few years back because they said I couldn't legally volunteer for a fashion show, I didn't know what was going to happen. And Trump was elected president, and because I was Muslim, maybe he'd be like, "Nah, she can't even get on the flight." Hell, I don't know. Anything could've prohibited me from getting to that speech. My stomach screamed at me.

Needless to say, I got on the flight. I didn't die. Trump hadn't interfered. I had a slight hiccup with customs; other than that, I was in Canada. Was this real? Was I really just flown out, all expenses paid. What had I done to deserve such a gift? An honor?

The phone at the hotel rang. It was the coordinator from the university making sure I was safe. Then she casually said that CBC wanted to interview me live on air. I dropped the phone.

"Leah?"

"Yup, I'm here still." I fanned myself. "When did they want me to come in? Will I be on camera? I'm afraid."

She chuckled. "Don't be scared. It's going to be okay. Just relax today, because tomorrow you'll have a full day. You'll have an assistant take you to the studios, then bring you here for the summit."

It was chilly that night, and usually I'd hibernate, but I was in a whole other country and wanted to sightsee and find some food. I walked around the downtown area before being picked up by one of my followers. She took me to this halal burger spot, and we chatted. She was sweet and had been following me for years. She even gave me this recycled fur key chain, which I thought was adorbs.

After she dropped me off, the night was still young, so I decided to go this random bar with a live band. Everybody in the bar was white. They all kinda looked at me like, what she doing in here? What they didn't know was that I was into all the '80s rock, and I fucked with all them white people bands like Velvet Revolver and Foo Fighters and Nine Inch Nails. I even dabbled in Marilyn Manson.

I bought a drink and sat alone and bobbed my head to the local band. They were pretty good. The next and last band was the hypest. I couldn't even stay in my seat. The front man was a midget with only three fingers on each hand, but he played that guitar as if he had about twenty fingers. His bass player was a bald fat man with a huge hillbilly beard and wore a rainbow-colored onesie. A student noticed me dancing alone and joined me. Then all her friends came over, and we rocked out. The odd Muslim girl and baby Canadian hippies.

I met up with my assigned assistant the next morning. Her job was to get me to all of the appointments on time and feed me. She was a chunky lady with blonde hair and said "eh" at the end of all her sentences. She was always checking her watch to make sure we stuck to the schedule. I could get used to this kind of lifestyle.

First stop, the CBC newsroom. It was so legit that we even had to get clearance before we entered. And it was huge! There were almost one hundred reporters in their short-walled cubicles, with their faces glued to their screens. The chatters blurred together like the buzzing of bees in a hive. Every time I walked past a cubicle, eyes would dart up, I guess wondering what I was doing there.

We were led to a waiting room. When the interviewer was done with his intro and segment, there would be a commercial break; then I'd have a few minutes to chat with him prior, then boom, we were going live.

Gurgle, gurgle.

Fuck.

"I'm going to go to lady's room real quick," I announced.

"Don't be too long," the blonde said. "Don't wanna miss your interview, eh?"

I nodded.

On the toilet, farts erupted. Air. But I knew there was more.

Before the interview, I found myself pacing back and forth. My assistant thought that by chatting my damn ear off, it would make me "less nervous." What she didn't know was that she was making me more nervous. My stomach twisted as I heard a pause. A lady peeked her head from around the corner. "You're up."

"Don't be nervous," the blonde reminded me.

Yes, I thought. Because someone telling you not to be nervous always helped.

I gave her a thumbs-up.

I shook the older white man's hand before I sat down. His palm was moist. He had a welcoming smile though.

He put his headphones on, and I put mine on. My hands shook.

"Nervous?" he said.

"Very," I replied.

"Ah, don't be."

I wanted to roll my eyes but that would be rude.

He counted down 3, 2, 1, and pointed to the staff behind me to start the recording.

My voice shook when he asked me the first question. I felt it. But then, I got a grip, and my stomach pains drifted away as I answered his questions about body positivity and why was I visiting Ottawa. At the end, he removed his headphones and stood. "Nervous? You are a natural."

I did a spin in my seat and said, "Well . . ."

The last appointment on the list was the actual event. My time slot was after lunch. And I wasn't on a panel like the rest of the participants. I had my own segment with an interviewer. I felt special. When I returned from the CBC newsroom to the large room on the top floor of the University of Ottawa, it seemed as if the crowd had tripled. All of the chairs were filled, and there were even people standing in the back. I walked in, and all attention was on me.

The coordinator hurried me to the stage, where my face surrounded the room in advertisements that they had posted all over campus. They all had come to see me. There were doctors and students and professors and speakers and artists. All Canadian and all from different cultures. I was in awe. My stomach began acting up, but it was showtime. They announced me. Then, on the big screen, they showed my "Muslim Girl Dance" video.

I'd never watched it with an audience before. I've actually never watched any of my work with an audience. While their fascination was geared to the music video, mine was geared toward their reactions to me. I shimmied my shoulders to the beat. Some of them mirrored me and shimmied too. I saw lowered jaws and wide eyes. I saw smiles and grins and elbow nudges.

I really had to hold in tears because I had on expensive eyeliner that I refused to smudge, and also I was making an impact, from something as shallow as modeling. Something as easy as dancing. I was a triple whammy: fat, Black, and Muslim in America. Showcasing my work at a summit about identity and owning your shit.

Those women (and men) had never seen anything like me before. I was a fat unicorn. A high-fashion unicorn. I'd fought against the odds to have a seat at that table. My very presence was breaking down stereotypes of what a Muslim looks like, what a fat girl looks like, what a Black girl looks like, what an unconventional, intersectional, and nonprivileged human looks like. When the video ended, I gave one of my infamous tongue pops and flipped my turban like it was hair, and the whole room of people rose from their seats, and applause and cheers rang in my ears.

This is exactly what I was meant to do.

EPILOGUE

I never wanted to share or write about myself, which is the reason why I majored in fiction and wrote dystopian fiction. My love for storytelling manifested in the way that I could safely show my true self in the form of a heroine, a villain, and all that in between. When you're someone like me, you find yourself hiding all the time, searching for the nearest shadow to disappear in. Concealing your truths and creating false narratives in order to protect yourself from the harshness, the prejudices of the world. And since beginning this journey, I've been subjected to all kinds of hate, projection, and ridicule, the very thing I was trying so hard to shield myself from. It's so much easier to hide, to agree, to not cause any trouble. Because when someone like me steps out of line and shouts, then the whole world shuts the fuck up and listens, and that's when the real change begins.

Somehow, I ended up taking a nonfiction class because I didn't have time for poetry, and I hadn't wanted to take playwriting. Nonfiction was going to be so boring, I thought. I was sure the professor was going to have us reading the greats—aka old white men from back in the day—and have us absorb it all and regurgitate back for a passing grade, like I'd done in my undergrad days.

The class was nothing like that. The very white professor had us read essays by contemporary African American writers. I was so ignorant that I hadn't even known Black people wrote so much creative nonfiction. He also wanted to hear our stories. Our personal narratives. Which made me quite uncomfortable. This meant that I had to out myself. Tell the truth about my feelings about my body, my mother's issues, my Muslim-ness. I wrote as he wished, making sure not to go too deep. I wasn't brave enough for that yet.

At the end of the semester, all students met with their class professor to go over their progress for that quarter. My professor was intimidating to me. I'd tell him jokes to make him smile, and he never did and would only shoot me slightly puzzled looks. He reminded me of someone that chuckled only once when watching some dry sitcom like *Frasier.* He wore circular frames and had thin salt-and-pepper hair. He had on a loose printed shirt, cargo shorts, and those heavy-duty dark-brown sandals worn by those old white guys who overly enjoy hiking.

We met inside a Starbucks at Barnes & Noble. Running late as usual, I scurried through the doors, out of breath, with a heavy backpack and scattered papers pinned to my chest. I gulped as his watery blue eyes bore into me. I knew he was going to tell me that I was the worst student he'd ever had and that I needed to stick with fiction.

"Leah, I'd just like to say that the stories about your mother are fascinating," he continued. "You have this knack for taking traumatic and painful and uncomfortable events and weaving them into this griping text that has a slight undertone of comedy, this lightheartedness."

As I picked my jaw up from the table, I said, "Umm, thank you."

"I know you are into fiction, but I would bet my career if I could persuade you to pursue nonfiction."

"I can't do that," I replied.

He finally shot me a laugh, the one I'd been fighting to get the entire semester. "Why?"

I shook my head. "I can't out my family. I can't out myself. With fiction, my secrets stay safe."

Years later, his prediction came true. During one of Michigan's worst winters, I found myself telling stories. My own stories. I wrote this book out of pure anger. I wrote this book to get it all out. I wanted to flush all the bad, the sins that were pent up inside of me after years and years and years of being told to shut up, be quiet, stop talking. When I was left alone, mangled to the core and unable to stand on my own, I went to what I knew. Telling stories.

With each story, I cried. I slammed the laptop down more times than I could count and took many naps from the exhaustion of recanting events that will never leave me. I've hit road blocks and backspaced memories too deep to share. Too incriminating to share in fear of looking like a bad person, a bad Black girl, a bad fat girl, a bad Muslim. This project has brought me more discomfort with each reading.

I'm afraid to even release it. There are times where I just want Google or Apple to create a time machine and go back and change my mind about writing these things, about submitting these stories, and signing a document saying that I'm totally okay with mass-producing it. That I'm totally okay with having people peek into my life for around twenty or so bucks.

There's this phrase I keep hearing throughout this publishing process: What's the takeaway from this? Why should people care?

And my initial answer was, I have no fuckin' clue. Granted, that's my initial reaction to a lot of things. Anyone can string to-gether a few words and slap "book" on it. But after sitting and pondering and allowing myself the understanding of the magni-tude, the importance of someone like me being vocal in America and beyond is insurmountable.

I had to shut out all the noise and just allow the words to flow freely without prejudice. I had to stop trying to be someone that I wasn't.

You know that popular saying: new year, who dis? This ideology that you have to become this new person with these brand-new ideas and have a new, carved-out body to be who you were truly meant to be. To live your best damn life. To get that perfect dude. To land that perfect job. That drastically changing yourself is the key to life's locked successes. This very ideology is what continues to keep us mentally confined.

I am not a new person. I am the same person that I've always been. My weight may fluctuate and my face may change due to age, but I am not a new person. And no matter what we do externally, we will always remain the same at our core.

I am not a new person, but I am an evolved person. I've listened more. Figured out what I like and what I don't like. I have been places and seen different things and experienced different people. I've unlocked something that no one expected me to unlock through my own evolution. Living in my own truths.

Through my own journey of self-awareness, I've unlocked the power of universality through experiential storytelling. Yes, I am fat, Black, Muslim, no daddy, divorced, educated, and a woman, but none of that matters because I am a human being first. Just like you. A being that thrives on connecting with other human beings. My entire platform has been built by just that. By ripping away all of those outer layers that divide us and toxic social constructs and connecting with humans on a human level, the most basic level. By just allowing them to share their story, allowing them a safe space in which to share what they've been concealing, what's heavy on their hearts. To allow them the voice that I wasn't allowed to have growing up, in my marriage, or in my very own community.

Societal norms on beauty and sexuality and religion have been placed upon us. We have inadvertently, generation to generation, carried these norms and supported them no matter how toxic. It's how we've always done it, they say. Well, I think it's time to do something different. The old ways no longer work. They no longer have a place in a more progressive world.

My wish is that through these stories, you find a newer way, a better way, a more humane way of tackling topics of color or weight or culture or otherness. As much as each essay has caused me great discomfort to read, to write, it has equally given me power. There is power in saying: this is me, unapologetically.

I am living, breathing proof that these created limits on body weight, color, socioeconomic status, height, religion carry not an ounce of real weight, an ounce of importance. Like one of my good friends always says, I am your permission slip. Through my stories, I am giving you permission—wherever you are—to do it. I encourage you to take that spark from my flame and reignite yours. And allow it to burn fiercely. Then allow someone else to take a spark from you to ignite theirs.

I feel like it took so long for me to arrive here, at this very moment with you. That I spent so much time trying to fit into what the standard was for beauty, what the standards are for a girl like me, that I've missed a whole chunk of life just floating around with not a clue of my identity, my impact.

I wish you could see what I see, feel what I feel, from the other side of self-acceptance, body acceptance. I hope that these stories—or at least one of them—has done that for you. Opened your eyes to something much deeper, something unexplored. This is only the beginning of so much more. I am truly frightened by the future, as I am emboldened by it.

On the days that I am tired, sick, frustrated, and ready to throw in the towel, I remind myself that I have covered territory that hasn't been covered yet and have more to cover. That my journey has become so much bigger than myself, my body. That it isn't about just me. The world needs to see my face, they need to see my body and all the rolls that come along with it. They need to hear my words. Because it's vital that we see marginalized bodies win and be included. I deserve a seat at the table as much as the next person despite my intersectionalities and because of my intersectionalities.

I remember when I first started blogging and modeling, my ex was so confused. He asked me why I felt the need to model. And then he reminded me that when you are married, your body belongs to your spouse.

I replied, "When you are an artist, your body belongs to the world."

ACKNOWLEDGMENTS

Wow. I have to write a whole-ass acknowledgments section. Why it came as a shock that I had to do this is beyond me. I mean, I barely thought I'd ever publish, let alone have to write about all the people who helped me get to this very moment. And when I tell you there are so many people, there are so many. I mean from people feeding me, buying me hookah when I was depressed, tossing one-hundred-dollar gigs my way, letting me sleep on their couches, lending me a shoulder to cry on, making me laugh when I ain't see nothing funny about life, gassing me (someone told me that I was their Beyoncé. Ha!).

I also toggled back and forth with being petty in this section. Should I name all the people that I thought was supposed to be there but weren't or told me I wasn't shit, that I wasn't going to make it to this point? As you've read my whole life story, I won't even waste the space on those individuals. Just know that I still thank those people, because without those harsh lessons, I surely wouldn't be here, on the other side of fear, of greatness.

So, I guess I'll start with thanking the younger version of myself. I am so incredibly thankful that the younger me didn't give up on a dream that many said wasn't possible. And although she believed them most of the time, she did it anyway. She had no clue what to expect, because someone like her had never seen anyone who looked like her accomplish the things she wanted in life. The representation that we have now, she didn't have. She held onto that hope, that dream that one day she'd get that one yes that she was waiting on. Through her resilience, her imperfections, her mental illness, through her rejection of self, and through the rejection of others and her humiliation because she was "weird" and not "Muslim enough," she persisted. With nothing but hope and a dream that she couldn't shake. And she tried to shake it; she let them go for many years, her talents and her goals, but one day they returned full circle, and she dove into that bitch wholeheartedly. And because of her, I am here.

I'd like to acknowledge the creator. I am not the most law-abiding religious Muslim you'll ever meet, but I'd like to say that I am spiritual. There were certain points where, on my knees, in tears on my prayer rug, I had to let the baggage go and give it to something higher than myself.

There's this popular saying that I live by: "What is meant for you will never pass you." I believe that with my entire being. That where I am, who I am, was already written and is just waiting for me to discover it.

Next would be my oldest sister, Tonisha, aka Taahira (her Muslim name). Although we are seven years apart and are totally different in every way, she has always been my rock, whether she knows this or not. Hadn't mattered if we were states apart, she always made herself available. She has bought me countless crab-leg dinners, hyped me up when I was at my lowest points, and chewed me out when necessary, and has the heart of gold and is the most understanding person you'll ever meet. Thank you for being my Big Sister and supporting me during our family's ridiculousness.

My fuckin' friends! They've seen me at my worst and at my highest and have celebrated every win with me—no matter how big or small. I have made so many tight bonds over the last few years. But I'll start with the mains, my sister-friends that have known me since I was mini Leah V.

Madinah, who is the kindest and most opinionated and stylish person (who also hooked my makeup up for the cover of this book. Ayyyeee). I used to think she was so cool when I was little. She's always been fearless when it came to turban wrapping and makeup. She has literally taught me everything I know about beauty. She has weathered the cold to take my OOTD photos, she has beat my face for free, and has assisted me on numerous sets. I honestly can't thank her enough for all that she's done. Like I'd have to give her a trillion dollars to repay her back for her kindness. We made it!

Asiyah, my very petty and loving handicapable friend who'd allow me to seek refuge at her house while I was going through my divorce. Our mothers were friends when we were young'uns, and it has grown into a sisterhood. I call her when I need to spill the "tea" or need dinner. I Facetime her when I experience the smallest inconvenience, and she cusses me out with love or gives me advice. Either way, she's always been in my corner.

My friend Laila, who is always the voice of reason and has the side-eye that would make anyone stop their nonsense, always calls to check up on my daily shenanigans. She makes me want to be less petty, and that's always a good thing.

I have to shout out my friends Mia, aka cat bae/all-night danceathon buddy; Jennifer, who's my second younger mom and makes sure I eat real meals; Layla, who makes sure I get my hookah fix; Brian, who graciously opened up his home to a freshly divorced social media influencer; Ramona, the vintage queen who literally forced me to model again when I said I was done; and Reima, who allowed me to connect with people from all over the world and believed in me, even when she hadn't even met me.

These are only a few people who have cussed me out while still encouraging me to make the leap or thrown me gigs or kind words to keep going: Ilyass, Lungi, Tiarra, Remy, RV, Tunde, Zuleyha, Jax, Amira, Siena, Uhshi, Aleksandra, Melissa, Daniella, Victoria, Huda, Malaika, Meghan, Alyonka, Ashley, Daniela (who shot the amazing cover), and to any of the names I missed, you are right here with me.

My agent, Penelope, aka P for short, because she's too cool. I had sent my book out to a hundred agents and editors in a forty-eight-hour period. My wrist was so sore, that's how much emailing I was doing. Immediately, thirteen agents replied, wanting to talk to me. Unheard of, my mentor said. I got so scared. Penelope was one of the last ones to reply. I took it down to six agents, then four, then two. I thank her for dealing with my angry cat GIFs that I send her when I'm freaking out over too many cuts or an email not replied to fast enough. She's patient and calm and gets down and dirty when needed. Thanks to all the folks at Gelfman Schneider/ICM Partners for representing my crazy ass.

Shout out to Beacon Press for housing my manuscript and Joanna Green for also taking into account my needs for how this book became this book. I appreciate your patience and guidance.

Huge acknowledgment to my writers of color who've paved the way for me to be right here: Issa Rae, Samantha Irby, Phoebe Robinson, Marlon James, Ava Duvernay, Roxane Gay.

Oprah. I've been obsessed with her since I was very young. She was a disadvantaged Black woman who was also plus-sized dominating the media. She was the one that I wrote papers on, who I thought was the human being that I and everyone else should aspire to be. I am here because of your courage.

My mentor, Taylor Polites, from Wilkes University, who took me from an eh writer to a va-va-voom writer with confidence and flair. I remember asking him, "What if white people get offended by my work?"

"Leah," he replied, "you don't write for white people. You don't write what's trendy. You write what you want to write. Everybody gets offended from something."

So, I wrote unapologetically ever since. He gave me permission to write as raw as I wanted.

To my Wilkes family, the creative writing faculty all the way down to the other master's students, thank you. My writers' groups, my class, who we spent hours online with trying to figure out if a sentence should go here or there, you, ladies and gents, you have made me a stronger writer indeed.

The hugest, most bottom of my heart, ugly face cry goes out to my social media community! Y'all are the bestest internet community I could ever have. Y'all go hard for me. Encourage me. Read my shit. Share my shit. Attack anyone that fucks with me. Bought webinars. Bought my little self-pub book and sent donations when I was too poor to pay my rent. A BIG THANK-YOU. I hope you enjoy this book the most. You've continuously inspired me to keep sharing my truths.

I can't leave without thanking my celebrity crushes. Cardi B, because I love seeing sexually liberated women of color who are also underdogs win. Slay Cardi! You keep people like me motivated. Queen RiRi, aka Rihanna, who shows me that you can be more than one thing. You can dominate as many fields as you want and at the same time sit on your security guard's shoulders and roll a blunt on his head while paparazzi snap photos. J. K. Rowling. I would not be a writer if it weren't for you and your journey. At that very moment of reading *Harry Potter*, I knew that I was going to pursue writing.

To my mother, who decided to be a mom, even though she had the weight of the world on her shoulders. We have definitely had our ups and downs, but you raised and protected me. That I could never repay you for. To my aunt Denise, who bought me my first *Harry Potter* book, which got me hooked on stories and how transformative characters could be. To my sassy late grandmother, who always dotted to her friends down South about the perfection of my eyebrow skills and showed off my blog.

Finally, to all the readers who still read, who still absorb words and take them as their own. Thank you for joining me on my journey. This was not easy to do. Like at all. But we did it. Thanks for spending your coins to support my dream, my baby, which is what you're cradling in your hands.

Thank you.